CRY
OF THE
HUMAN
HEART

Creation House is a ministry of Christian Life Missions. Its purpose is to publish and distribute Bibles, books and other Christian literature presenting the gospel of Jesus Christ. If you would like additional information, we encourage you to write to us at 396 E. St. Charles Rd., in Wheaton, IL 60187.

CRY
OF THE
HUMAN
HEART

Juan Carlos Ortiz

CREATION HOUSE
CAROL STREAM, ILLINOIS

CRY OF THE HUMAN HEART
by Juan Carlos Ortiz

Foreign Translations

British	Marshall, Morgan & Scott 1 Bath Street London EC1V9LB England
Dutch	Uitgevery Gideon Dorpsweg 57 4223 NC Hoornaar Holland
Finnish	Kustannuskeskus PAIVA OY Lukiokatu 15 D Kristillista Kirjallisuutta Finland
German	Missionsverlag Sieg des Kreuzes Lutt Kollau 17 D 2000 Hamburg 61, Germany
Norwegian	Ansgar Forlag Mollergatan 26 Oslo, Norway
Swedish	Libris Box 1623 S 701 16 Orebro Sweden

© 1977 by Juan Carlos Ortiz. All rights reserved.
Published by Creation House, 396 E. St. Charles Rd., Carol Stream, Illinois 60187.

Scriptures used are the author's free translations unless otherwise indicated.
Biblical quotations from the **New American Standard Bible** © 1971 are used with permission from the Lockman Foundation.
Printed in the United States of America.

First Printing, April, 1977
Second Printing, April, 1978
Third Printing, August, 1980
Fourth Printing, March, 1982
Fifth Printing, March, 1984
ISBN 0-88419-010-2
Library of Congress Catalog Card Number 76-24099

Contents

1

Two Kingdoms

When I first went to Japan, I found myself in a foreign world. Their faces appeared different. Their writing is different. They are in a completely different culture. They bathe together, but they eat alone in the restaurants.

When you go to a Japanese restaurant, they give you a little room for yourself, and you eat in private. But when you bathe, you bathe with everybody! In Argentina, we eat with everybody and we bathe in private.

So many things were different that I found myself feeling very strange. I liked it very much, but I felt strange.

One day in Japan, behind me I heard a voice saying, *"Dios te bendiga, hermano."* "God bless you, brother." Spanish in Japan! It was a Japanese Christian behind me, who recognized me.

"I am Mexican," he explained. "I was born in Mexico. My parents were Japanese and they emigrated to Mexico. I was saved in Mexico and they sent me here as a missionary to Japan."

From that day on, we were together. I had an interpreter and we were always speaking Spanish together. It was wonderful!

Listen. We are in a foreign world. We belong to another kingdom than the one we reside in. When we meet someone who belongs also to our kingdom, that is a happy thing!

To understand our situation of living in two kingdoms, we need to try to change our frame of reference. Perhaps this is one of the most difficult things to do. What do I mean by a "frame of reference"?

We are living in a certain situation. We belong to a Pentecostal church, perhaps, in a Lutheran country. Or we are baptized-in-the-Spirit Methodists, and we have many denominations around us. We have some truth within us. So we have a frame of reference. And everything we hear, we judge it according to our frame of reference.

I don't claim that I have God's frame of reference. I know that God's frame of reference is much greater than mine.

I have this little frame of reference. If something comes along that is outside of it, I say it is "from the devil." I can't understand it, so it is wrong.

So what is God's frame of reference? Even though I don't claim to know *all* of God's frame of reference, I will try to probe it a little. We are going to speak about the kingdom of God. Jesus said, "If you are not born again, you cannot enter into the kingdom of God." The first question we have is, what is the kingdom of God? Even if I cannot understand it in its fulness, at least I have to know something about it.

For some people, the kingdom of God is the Pentecostal Church. For some others, the Catholic Church is the kingdom of God, or the charismatic kingdom is the kingdom of God.

But what does the Bible say is the kingdom of God?

And He is the image of the invisible God, the first born of all creation. For in Him all things were created, both in the heavens and on earth, visible and invisible, whether thrones or dominions or rulers or authorities — all things have been created through Him and for Him.

And He is before all things, and In Him all things hold together. He is also head of the body, the church; and He is the beginning, the first-born from the dead; so that He Himself might come to have first place in everything.

For it was the Father's good pleasure for all the fulness to dwell in Him, and through Him to reconcile all things to Himself, having made peace through the blood of His cross; through Him, I say, whether things on earth or things in heaven.

And although you were formerly alienated and hostile in mind, engaged in evil deeds, yet He has now reconciled you in His fleshly body through death, in order to present you before Him holy and blameless and beyond reproach — if indeed you continue in the faith firmly established and steadfast, and not moved away from the hope of the Gospel that you have heard, which was proclaimed in all creation under heaven, and of which I, Paul was made a minister.

Colossians 1: 15-23 NASB

What is the kingdom of God? The whole universe: all the things that God created. Jesus is the First of all things, and God is the Maker, Owner and King.

We are too conscious of our little earth. What is it? Just a small little marble that travels around the sun with other planets. But God's kingdom is much bigger than that. You know the solar system is a family of planets with a sun for a daddy. But every star is a sun and can have planets around it. In all this galaxy that we belong to, the Milky Way, there are millions and millions of suns. Our sun is one of the smaller stars. We see it as big because it is closer, but this Milky Way is a tremendous galaxy. We are told that to go from one star to its neighbor star, and these are very close, it would take 80,000 years of travel in our fastest rocket. Eighty-thousand years between neighboring stars! Then how much would it take to travel from one end of the Milky Way to the other?

And the Milky Way is just one of the galaxies. We belong to a family of ten galaxies, and some of these are bigger than the Milky Way. Then this is not the only family of galaxies, there are millions of families of galaxies.

And all were created by Him and for Him! And who says that the galaxies are the only thing that He created? Perhaps the galaxies are just the garden of the palace, and we know nothing about the palace and the backyard!

It's a tremendous creation — the whole kingdom of God. And God did not create the universe to play marbles with. He had a purpose. He put inhabitants in the universe.

And God not only created material, visible things. Paul says that God made thrones, dominions, principalities, powers, all things were created by Him and for Him, visible or invisible. So in this universe there are thrones, systems of government, dominions, principalities, and all those powers are under King Jesus.

Jesus is much, much more than your personal Savior, He has much more to do. He must be somewhere in the heavens in His central office with all the controls and switches there. Because all things were created by Him and for Him and by Him all things hold together. He is the Maintainer, the Sustainer of all things. The whole universe depends on Him. By Him all things consist.

Where does He have his "office"? Some people say it is in the third heaven. I was told in seminary that the first heaven was where the planes fly, the second heaven is where the galaxies are. And the third heaven is where God is. And that is all. Perhaps that is right. Perhaps not. Perhaps the first heaven is where the galaxies are, the second we know nothing about, the third is where Jesus has his "office," and there may be many other heavens.

Paul went to the third heaven. He got access to the central offices of God. I don't know if he went to the very central head office. Perhaps he was taken only to the Milky Way department. But by the vision of the Church he had, I understand that he was taken very far.

Someone says, "What a vision my pastor had! He built a church for 300 people! What a vision! He bought an organ and he is going to put a carpet on the floor. What a vision! This man thinks that Jesus is looking only at his little church.

He thinks that in heaven God gives his full attention only to his little group, saying, "Looook! Look at the meeting they have. How nice."

Some other pastors have a vision for a city. Those are the servants whom Jesus has taken to the mountain outside the city and said, "Look at the city! Look at My church — all divided!"

Some others gain a vision for more than the city, but Paul had a vision of the Church in the context of the whole universe. He says that the Church is going to show the manifold wisdom of God to the principalities and powers in the heavens.

So Paul had a greater vision. He was in the third heaven and saw the blueprints. That is the reason why he was a master builder. A master builder is one who has access to the blueprints. We need people today that have access to the central office of God and see the blueprints for the church.

So Jesus has to do with the whole universe. We understand that at one time there were some problems in the kingdom of God. We don't know too much about it, but we know something because of this holy Book. We know that one day part of the universe rebelled against God. There was a split. We don't know who was the leader of the split. Some people think that Lucifer was. Probably. I don't want to give him too much importance.

You know what Smith Wigglesworth, the Englishman who saw so many miracles of God, said in one of his anecdotes. Wigglesworth was sleeping and suddenly he felt his bed being moved. He felt that somebody was at the foot of the bed, so he lit a candle and looked and it was Lucifer sitting there. "Oh, it's only you," he said and went back to sleep. Alleluia!

So I don't want to give him too much importance. But according to the Revelation, Satan drew after him in his rebellion a third of the stars. We don't know if that expression is symbolical or spiritual or literal. It could be many things. But some parts of the universe rebelled against God, of that we are sure. We know that there is a kingdom of darkness today. Part of God's kingdom was split and that part became the kingdom of darkness. Satan is very experienced in splits. He is a specialist there. He can split the family, or a church, or the kingdom of God.

Satan is called "the prince of this world." When the Bible speaks of "principalities and powers," it may be referring to wicked angels who rule over the nations. There is the Prince of Persia in Daniel 10:13, who prevented the answer to Daniel's prayers. Paul says we do not fight with flesh and blood, but with principalities, powers, rulers of the darkness of this world, spiritual wickedness in high places (Ephesians 6:12).

Perhaps over a whole planet is a prince, and Satan then is the prince of the whole earth. So if this is the case, perhaps our earth was the capital city of the rebellion, because here lives the one who made the rebellion. It may be that this is the headquarters of the rebellion because Jesus said that we are near to the gates of hell. If this is the capital city of the rebellion, there was the reason why the cross had to come to this planet.

So perhaps all the stars and galaxies near ours belong to the kingdom of darkness, if we are in the midst of that part of God's kingdom that was rebelling against God. That is the reason why Paul said we are not fighting flesh and blood, but principalities and powers of the air. That is the reason why our work here is not so easy. All around us is enemy territory.

We are where Satan has his headquarters. Who knows? When Satan has his cabinet meetings, how many princes come to this earth? How many wicked spirits come from different parts of the universe to meet with him here? And we are right in the midst of the rebellion, in the capital city where Satan started all this, in the midst of the kingdom of darkness.

So should we sit down and resign ourselves to inevitable defeat? Absolutely not! We have only heard half of the story. The best is now to come.

2

Christ and the Kingdom of God

One day God saw that the time had come to put into effect some plans laid before the foundation of the world. This situation with people and a third of His universe alienated from Himself could no longer go unchallenged. He acted to recover what was lost and bring it under His authority again.

I am very touched by the way God planned to bring it all under Him again. He appointed His Son, Jesus Christ, to recover, to make conquest of this part which had rebelled against God and to bring it back into His kingdom. We read in I Corinthians 15 that Jesus was made King until He would subdue everything under His feet. Then when everything is submitted under Jesus Christ, He will give the kingdom to the Father, and God will be all in all.

I don't know when Jesus received this special commission. But I think it happened after His resurrection. Remember that then Mary wanted to touch Him, and He said, "No, don't touch Me, because I have to go to My Father."

Of course, later He took the official cloud to heaven. But before He went officially, He took a quick trip unofficially. I think that then God gave Him the power to act in God's name and with all of God's authority to bring His part of the kingdom back.

Then Jesus came to His disciples and said, "All authority has been given to Me in heaven and on earth. Go therefore and make disciples" (Matthew 28:18, 19 NASB). He told these people here on earth to go because He had authority over all things, and He was the One to bring everything back to God.

I am amazed and very touched by the way He did it, and is doing it. He used the way of peace because He is the King of Peace. He wanted to bring all this back to God, not by coercion, not by punishment, but by love and reconciliation. God wanted "to reconcile all things to Himself ... whether things on earth or things in heaven visible or invisible" (Colossians 1:20 NASB), so He appointed Jesus.

This marvelous Jesus, the first thing He did was to pay the price of reconciliation. What is to be done if two people are at odds because one of them has a debt to the other one that he can't pay?

Not long ago I was facing a problem. One missionary lady had come home from the mission field and she owed a missionary man $100, and I was called in to settle the situation. It was very difficult. He said she should pay the $100.

She said, "I can't, and I don't think I should pay it. I was working under you when I made that expense."

"No, that was for your dentist," he said. "You have to pay me."

"I was on the mission field," she told me, "working under him and he should pay for my teeth."

Neither would give in. I thought for a moment, then I pulled out my wallet.

I said, "I am going to trade you your problem for another one. I will pay the debt." I said to him, "There is the $100. What are you going to do now?" I said to her, "You don't owe him any more. You have no rights to claim now. What are you going to do?"

They looked at each other and started to weep. She was not expecting that I would pay the $100. I usually never have $100 in my pocket. My salary in Argentina is $150 a month. I had it there because I was just coming home from a trip. They were not expecting it, so they were touched. In my country $100 is a lot of money. Workers earn $50 a month.

At last they hugged each other. They could do nothing else because the debt was paid.

Jesus was told by God, "Bring those rebellious people back under Me." So He came to this earth and paid for the reconciliation. There is now nothing against us before God. Jesus has died for us and God will receive in His arms all those who accept this Savior, this Lord who came in God's name to bring us the message of reconciliation.

Now we belong to the kingdom of God because we have been born again. But physically we are still in the enemy's territory. Geographically, we are still in Satan's kingdom. You know that *geo* means earth, so I mean that on this earth and in the nearby heavens there is rebellion.

This is the reason we do not understand some of the things that happen here. If God is good, why wars? Why floods? Why earthquakes? Why this accident? Why were little children killed? Why the blind people? Why the lame people? Why the poverty? *Why?* Don't forget, physically we are not in God's kingdom. God's kingdom is righteousness, peace and joy, and no whys!

Even though we don't belong to this world, we are in this world. Even Jesus accepted it when Satan showed Him all the kingdoms of this world and said, "All these are mine, and I give them to whoever I want to give them, so worship me and I will give them to You" (Luke 4:5, 6). Jesus did not accept that option because He had a better one. He knew the way. All things were under Him.

But Satan and his senior governors are responsible for things that happen in this black part of the universe, and this is called the kingdom of darkness. What do you have in the kingdom of darkness but darkness, hatred, wars and famines?

We are living like the children of Israel in the land of Goshen during the plagues. All around us are problems and death. But we have light when they have darkness. Alleluia! We have peace when they have war, because God's kingdom is in our hearts. But this earth is going to pass away because it still belongs to the kingdom of darkness.

I have no problem with catastrophes. Some people say, "How come, if God is good, that cyclone came to Australia?" "Why was there war in Korea and Vietnam and hunger in Biafra and Ethiopia? Why?"

Dear brothers, we are in the midst of the kingdom of darkness, and you know Satan is crazy. He has problems and rebellion worse than the social situation in my country. Darkness is being found in many of the top men of government around the world. Satan can use all the Mafia there are, and all the secret things we do not know to conquer the world and prepare for the Antichrist. This is the kingdom of darkness.

Jesus knew where He was setting up His kingdom. For

those who came to Him, He prayed, "Father, I ask you to keep them from the world, not to take them out of it, but to keep them from the evil one" (John 17:15). All this earth is under condemnation and darkness. He knew that we could not expect nice things from it while it is under the rulership of Satan.

But the King came in Person into this darkness. As John said, "In Him was life; and the life was the light of men. And the light shines in the darkness; and the darkness did not comprehend it" (John 1:4, 5). He came and light erupted into the darkness, and the darkness has never put it out (Phillips).

The singing of the angels when Jesus was born meant that God has good will toward man. They said that God wants peace to be on earth and the good will of God to all men. The good will was that the kingdom of God come closer to this kingdom of darkness.

The first thing announced by John the Baptist on this earth was: "Repent, for the kingdom of heaven is at hand" (Matthew 3:2 NASB). You can imagine what a tremendous hope this was for alienated people. There were no embassies of the kingdom of God in the kingdom of darkness, no consulates. It was impossible to get a passport or a visa to go out. Satan would not let anybody pass through that darkness curtain. It was much heavier than any iron or bamboo curtain.

Also, God doesn't make it very easy to get into His kingdom. You have to be born there to belong. He doesn't accept immigrants or tourists. So it is a difficult situation. God is very wise and He made only one requirement. To get into His kingdom a person must be born again into that kingdom. He cannot pass the border just because he has a friend in it. No, no, no. We won't get in because we are intelligent, or schooled, or rich. No way. It is by birth only that we enter the kingdom.

And God is wise in that. Suppose I wanted to become an Australian citizen, and I went to the authorities and asked to be naturalized. Even though I would get the citizenship, always deep in my heart there would be a remembrance of Argentina — of those two-pound steaks for 50¢, and of my Spanish language. God doesn't want that at all. He wants us to be wholly of His kingdom, fanatics of His kingdom.

So He doesn't accept residents or immigrants or people who are naturalized. You must be born in that kingdom, and this is not so easy. It is not so easy to get free of Satan. He won't let you go easily to the other kingdom. The only way you can get free of him is by death. Yes, if you die you can. So that is what Jesus did. He provided a death for us. Alleluia!

Just look to the blood of Jesus and you die.

Satan says, "Where is Johnny?"

"He died."

"But he was very healthy."

"Yes, but he looked to the blood of Jesus."

The blood is here in the midst of the darkness, available to all. The cross is the hope. Just a look of faith at the blood, and even if you don't understand the concept, it is a touch of Jesus, so you die. His death is for everybody in the kingdom of darkness. Anyone can experience the power of the blood and get rid of the kingdom of darkness.

And the same Jesus who provided the death has provided a resurrection and a new life. The message of the cross is only half, or less than half, for without the resurrection we have nothing. We are dead in Him, and we are resurrected in Him, so we are born again, by faith in Him.

So the situation when Jesus came was this, He came to the capital city of the kingdom of darkness so that He could plant His kingdom in the hearts of those who would repent and believe.

When Jesus was to be crucified, Pilate asked Him, "Are

you the King of the Jews?"

Jesus answered, "But my kingdom is not of this world" (John 18:33, 36). Where does He put His kingdom then? "The kingdom of God is within you" (Luke 17:21 KJV). To those who receive Him, He gave power to become the sons of God (John 1:12). The kingdom is established in the inner parts of man. Not in the White House in Washington, not in a king's palace, but in the heart of every man who opens that heart to Him.

When a person opens his heart, Jesus comes to rule. That person is under Him, so he belongs to the kingdom of God even if his feet are still in the kingdom of darkness. We have to open, then Jesus comes within us and rules for us. This is to come back to the right King. Jesus Christ is the King that God has appointed. Repent! Repent of your rebellion and believe the good news. The price is paid.

Come.

3

The Diaper Set

Now we have something very sad in the Church today. Too many of the called-out people do not behave like called-out people. Often they behave almost the same as when they were in the kingdom of darkness — the kingdom they were supposed to leave behind. In the Church under the surface we find jealousy, quarreling, competition, resentment, lack of love, apathy and selfishness.

The lack of love in the Church, the lack of fruit for God, the lack of spiritual power, is not because believers are rebellious. They are not bad, or wrong or naughty. It is simply that they are underdeveloped. They are babes. They cannot do more or love more; they cannot give more or evangelize more, not because they are rebels, but because they are babies. That is the complaint of the apostles about the Christians in the early Church.

> . . . You have become dull of hearing.
> For though by this time you ought to be teachers, you have need again for someone to teach you the elementary principles of the oracles of God, and you have come to need milk and not solid food.
> For every one who partakes only of milk is not accustomed to the word of righteousness, for he is a babe.
> But solid food is for the mature, who because of practice have their senses trained to discern good and evil.
> Hebrews 5:11-14 NASB
> And I, brethren, could not speak to you as to spiritual men, but as to men of flesh, as to babes in Christ.
> I gave you milk to drink, not solid food; for you were not yet able to receive it. Indeed, even now you are not yet able. . . .
> I Corinthians 3: 1,2 NASB

"Babes in Christ." "You are still babes." Who is responsible for this condition? Are the babes themselves guilty? Are pastors guilty? Are the structures of the church guilty, or our theological traditions? Well, we are not going to try to find out who is guilty, but we will seek to find a solution for this problem.

First, if we really want to be open to God, we will humble ourselves and recognize this spiritual underdevelopment. If we are not ready to leave the bottle, the pacifier and the diapers, we cannot grow. We need to recognize the structures that are made for children, for what they are.

When I was a little boy, I went to what we call in Argentina "Children's City." It is a place where everything is small. The streets and houses fit children just right. I enjoyed so much to go there.

But now, when I take my children, I cannot get into those little buildings I liked so much—the post office, the hospital, the tiny dining rooms. I would have to bend very low to get in, because they stayed the same size while I grew up.

This happens with structures. Usually they are rigid and static, but life is dynamic and growing. Any person who grows a little bit will bump his head against the ceiling of the structure, and problems start.

We need to be ready for changes, ready for dynamic and growing relationships in a dynamic and growing community of the called out. Are we ready for the new community which is going to be the result of the move of the Spirit upon all flesh, giving life, the real life of the kingdom of God? Let's open our eyes to recognize our underdeveloped state and trust His life in us for new growth.

What tells us that we are really babes? First of all, our dependency on others rather than on God. We are always asking for prayers, always needing pastoral visits, always needing comfort. We are always looking for someone to take care of us. That is dependence.

In seminary pastors are trained in pastoral theology to maintain people as babes. One must visit them and keep them entertained. But the purpose of believers is not to be entertained in the congregations until they die in the grace of God! We must grow up and develop and become ministers ourselves. Pastors are to prepare the saints for the work of the ministry, not to entertain them. They are not caretakers of a brick pile, but builders of a building!

People come and say, "Pastor, I have a problem. My mother-in-law moved into our house. I don't know what to do."

"All right, I will pray for you. Lord, help him in this

problem. Amen. Good-bye."

Another comes, "Pastor, I have a pain here."

"I will pray for you and come to visit you."

That's like when a little boy comes to his dad, "Daddy, look! I have a hurt here."

Daddy says, "Pain, pain, go away; come again some other day."

"Thank you, Daddy."

If we continue our traditional type of visiting and counseling, we won't change the situation. Our religious institutions often look more like a hospital than an army. The pastor has to go from bed to bed asking, "How are you, brother? How do you feel? That's nice!"

We need to be soldiers in the kingdom of God. If there is a forest in the way, soldiers cut the trees. If there is a river, soldiers make a bridge. If there is a mountain, they dynamite it, but they have to go on. Soldiers cannot afford the luxury of having problems.

This is what Jesus meant when He said, "Come to Me, all who are weary and heavy-laden, and I will give you rest. Take My yoke upon you" (Matthew 11: 28,29 NASB). He was saying, I will take your yoke from you in order to put on you My yoke. He will then free us of all failure and all that obsession with ourselves and our things, for we choose to seek first the kingdom of God and His righteousness. We now bear, not ours, but Jesus' problems, Jesus' burdens, the interests of the kingdom of God.

This changes the way we counsel people. When one says, "Pray for me, I've lost my job," we answer him, "I can't pray for you as I used to."

"Why not?"

"I will believe with you for another job. Now go hit the pavement."

The writer to the Hebrews says that by this time you ought to be what? Teachers. You ought to be spiritual fathers taking care of children, but instead you still come for diapers, bottles, pacifiers and talcum!

Brother Ortiz, isn't that too hard? Well, what do you want to make—hospital patients or soldiers of the kingdom?

One came to Jesus and said, "I am following you, but *first* let me bury my father."

"Wait a moment!" Jesus said. "Who are you putting ahead of Me? Let the dead bury the dead. You follow Me."

John speaks about three kinds of people who have entered the kingdom. He says,

> I am writing to you, little children, because your sins are forgiven you for His name's sake . . .
> I am writing to you, young men, because you have overcome the evil one . . .
> I have written to you, fathers, because you know Him who has been from the beginning.
>
> 1 John 2: 12-14 NASB

These are three different levels of spiritual growth, not of physical age. The young men have overcome the devil. One may be eighty years old and still not have overcome the wicked one. So John is not talking about physical age.

As a matter of fact, most of the epistle is directed to "little children." That phrase is repeated over and over until the last verse of the book, "Little children, guard yourselves from idols" (1 John 5:21 NASB). But there were some there who were growing and some who were grown up.

"Little children" are the ones who are dependent on others. They do not produce anything; they only receive. Other people have to spend time and money on them.

"Young men" produce, but just enough for themselves. Usually when a boy gets his first job, he wants to buy his car and his clothes. Only when he becomes a father does he produce for others, usually for his children and family. Young men are strong, they have overcome the wicked one, and the Word of God abides in them. Eventually they get married and have children and feed them. And so it is spiritually.

I have some "fathers" in my congregation now. Some of my people would be offended if I came to visit them. "No, please," they would say, "what do you think? That I am a little child?" Now they believe in visiting the pastor!

Where do pastors and leaders go when they need help? Usually pastors depend on books, Sunday school materials, cassettes, video-tapes, and conventions to get new ideas, methods, and mechanics. If we really want our people to be dependent upon God, we will start to have fellowship with God and to receive the solid food from Him for our people. We won't want to give out secondhand material and leftovers. We will have fresh food we have received for them through the Spirit within us.

Materialism is another indication of childhood. Why are people materialistic? Not because they have rebelled. Children are materialistic by nature. Children do not know the value of things.

If spiritual things have little value, and material things do, it is because we lack the ability to value things properly. If a new car every year is more important than the mission field and expanding the kingdom, it is either because people are crazy or they are children. If we minister the kingdom of God to people and demonstrate what overcoming in the kingdom could mean for mankind, they will run to give up all they are and all they have. They will seek that kingdom first, knowing that all the other things will be added.

Why do we seek those "other things"? Because they have not been added to us. And why have they not been added? Because we are not seeking first the kingdom.

The very fact that we continually have to ask for prayer for healing and blessings shows that we are not seeking first the kingdom. So don't pray for them, but seek the kingdom first. Learn to grow.

One says, "Brother, I have a pain here."

"I'll pray for you."

"Now I feel better."

But soon he comes again to say, "Oh, now the pain is over here!"

Listen, you won't have so many pains if you seek God's kingdom first. Seeking your own kingdom brings on some of these problems.

I am learning this, dear friend, by experience. As best I can remember, for the last five years I have seldom or never asked something like that from God. I believe that while I am seeking first the kingdom of God and His righteousness, all these other things will be added unto me. I have never had more than I have now, and I don't ask for it.

Of course, God is very wise. He is smart. If I am living completely for His kingdom, then it is in His interest that I am healthy and have good food, and everything else I need, because I have given myself completely to Him. So if I fail, His interests suffer. God is very smart. Alleluia!

This we will want to tell other people too. Do not give them the "other things" when they come for them. Tell them that the root of their problem is that they are not seeking first the kingdom. But they should seek first the government of God, seek to expand and strengthen His kingdom, and seek His righteousness, and forget about the other things.

Look at my car. It does not worry about the gas, the oil, or the water. That's up to me. The car's business is to take me where I want to go. Never does a car say, "Why don't you put in some gasoline? I want some oil. Hey! put in some fuel!" Never.

When I drive it, the car never says to me, "No, not through that mud!"

"But that's what I want."

"I'll get dirty there!"

"It doesn't matter."

"Will you wash me?"

"That's up to me. You just take me where I'm going."

I take care of the gas, oil, water, washing, waxing, everything. That's up to me, not to it.

So it is with God. He cares for my vitamins and my proteins. He knows. He made me. He knows how much I need of everything. If I am living completely for Him, the best thing He can do is to maintain me in good shape, in shape for His kingdom.

This we will be anxious to tell others. No more should we inject sedative prayers just to relieve the pain for a moment instead of curing the cause of the illness. What hope is there for permanent relief if our people do not grow? No hope. Our only hope is to see the light and get the solid food that God wants to give us.

4

Children Quarrel

When I was a little boy, a preacher came to our church who had a nice, long beard. Beards were not common in those days and I fell in love with the beard. So in the secret of my heart, I started to pray and fast for a beard like his. I was eight years old.

One day while I was fasting, my mother said, "Aren't you going to eat, Johnny?"

"No, Mommy, I'm fasting."

"What is the reason, son?"

"It's a secret prayer to the Lord."

I didn't tell the reason for my fast, but the beard did not come. When I was sixteen, the beard came without fasting. I grew up, that's all. Often what we lack can only come by growth!

29

Children look at things as they appear on the outside. Give a child two boxes, one big and one small, and he will choose the bigger one. Even though the small package may contain something much better, the child will choose the bigger one because he looks only at externals.

Believers who are spiritually immature also tend to get hung up on externals. We see external sins so clearly and inner sins almost not at all. God wants us to be sanctified —spirit, soul and body. But we usually make an issue only of the things of the flesh: sex, alcohol, tobacco, drugs, the way we dress, etc. The sins we do not deal with are of much more consequence. Moreover, if we do not overcome the inner sins, we will never get rid of the surface ones either.

By inner sins, I mean sins of the soul, like pride. I have never seen a brother disciplined or separated from the Lord's Table because he was proud. If he would smoke, yes, but he could be the most arrogant person around and not be disciplined. Factions, ambition and the abuse of power, these are sins also, as is stubbornness. Jealousy is one of the worst sins in the church, especially among leaders, but we never deal with that. We are working on fornication, adultery, and drinking wine, even though all these sins are on the same level.

But look even deeper than these sins. There are sins of the spirit in the innermost part of man: the sins of the conscience, and disobedience to the inner voice of the Spirit. Our obedience to God does not consist only in keeping the written commandments, but in saying a wholehearted yes to the promptings of the King who lives within.

The King is a Person, not a book on the table, but a Person who lives inside. Living with Him goes beyond the book. Moses was told to speak to the rock. Instead, he smote the rock. Water came, and none of us would have judged him. He wouldn't have been disciplined in church.

But he knew what God had told him, and he did it his own way and was disciplined by God.

You can easily tell by my name that I am Spanish. But my wife had grandparents from England, so we gave our children English names. Once we were on a retreat with a group of other pastors, and the others were calling their boys: "Marcos!" "Antonio!" "Luis!"

I was calling, "Robert John, come here!"

The Spirit said, "That's wrong."

I went to the prayer room and asked, "Why is it wrong?"

"Why do you call your children in English when you are an Argentine and everybody here is Spanish? Does it give you some higher status, or what? Why not call him Roberto Juan, at least in this country?"

"Forgive me, Lord. Thank you."

Of course, nobody would discipline me for calling my children in English. My wife continues to call our son Robert John. The Spirit didn't say anything to her.

But He said it to me. I do not understand it very well, but I joyfully do it. If I refused, it would be the same as if I would commit fornication, because I would be disobeying God's voice.

What other problems result from our tendency to look more at externals? I think that racism and divisions in the Church show that we are looking only at the outside. Some people think God made black people to serve white people. They even find Bible verses to "prove" their point. They say that Noah cursed Canaan by making him to be a servant of his brothers. From Canaan came all Africans, so God must have meant them to be slaves! Of course, they forget that when Jesus died on the cross, He lifted all curses, and that in the kingdom of God there is no Jew nor Gentile, no male nor female, no black nor white. The new creature in Christ is what counts.

Quarreling and divisions come naturally to children.

Paul says, "And I, brethren, could not speak to you as to spiritual men, but as to men of flesh, as to babes in Christ. ... For since there is jealousy and strife among you, are you not fleshly, and are you not walking like mere men?" (1 Corinthians 3:1, 3 NASB).

A person who leaves the Episcopalians because he opposes them is really freed from nothing. I know people who became charismatics and started to criticize their former denomination. Before, they used to criticize the charismatics!

God must have been glad when He saw the Episcopalian open his heart to the Pentecostal brother. "At last!" God whispered. But when the man passed to the other side and went on criticizing as before, God must have said, "Oh, he's just the same!" He just changed sides, but he gained nothing in the knowledge of God. The kingdom of God gained nothing.

Many people are against all denominations, but they have their own groups. They say, "At last we are delivered from the denominations!" But their small, exclusive groups are caught up with their own interests just as the large groups from which they came. The groupist spirit that follows us is very hard to get rid of. It is like a fatal growth attached to us.

We are called to renew our spirits. When we meet somebody, we try to determine if he is renewed. If he is not renewed, we think, *Poor man!* So then we have the "renewed" and the "not renewed," those who have the vision and those who don't.

So the groupist spirit among Christians is a real problem. The way in which we have divided ourselves is childish.

"Who is this group?"

"They are Pentecostal."

"And the group next to them, are they not also speaking in tongues?"

"Yes, but they dance in the Spirit, and the others don't."

One separated group has elders instead of pastors, and the next is against drinking wine. And on and on it goes. We act like little children out to play. Our "isms" must look silly to the angels.

A man who wanted to buy a farm was looking it over. He found the cows divided into little groups.

"Tell me why you have divided the cows like this," said the man.

"Well," said the farmer, "these cows here are all white."

"Yes, I see that, but those are also white."

"Those have shorter legs."

"But the cows over there are white and have short legs, too. Why are they separate?"

"Oh, they have longer horns."

"Well! When I buy this farm, I will divide the cows into just two groups: those who give milk and those who don't."

The cause of all these problems is not rebellion. It is lack of spiritual growth. Our religious structures keep us immature.

All are caught up in the same thing, because we are children—Pentecostal children, charismatic children, Episcopal children—but children.

Sometimes I take one of my children downtown.

I say, "I'll buy you an ice cream cone, but please don't tell your brothers when you get home."

"Yes, Daddy."

So my son eats the ice cream, and the first thing he says when we get home is, "Daddy bought me an ice cream and it was big like this!"

It's too late then to remind him because already four other children have begun quarreling with him and me!

Believers who receive special blessings often treat them like a child treats an ice cream cone. Someone gets up to give a testimony.

"Well, while I was sitting there, I saw a light!"

"What did you do?"

"I saw a light. It was big like this."

And already another person in the congregation is thinking, *I didn't see a light. Why did God give him a light and not me?* When we treat blessings like this, we are hindered from receiving more.

God would like to give us more, but He does not because He loves us. To give us more would spoil us.

When I was a babe, I said, "Give me all the gifts, please, God. I want the gift of healing, the gift of faith, the gift of . . ."

Now I say, "Please, God, do not give me any gift, and do not give them to those I know. You know we would use them badly without a clear vision of the kingdom of God. One would use it to enlarge the charismatic kingdom. Another would use it to enlarge the Baptist kingdom. But until we receive the mind of Christ and the understanding of the kingdom of God, please, God, we have enough."

Just to show He is alive, God does give a miracle here and there. He gives one to the Foursquare, and a miracle to the Baptists, and another to the Catholics, but He hasn't yet poured out all His power without measure as He could, because He doesn't want us to try to use His power to strengthen our little kingdoms. If we have tongues, prophecies, miracles, and faith to transplant mountains, but have no love, we are nothing. The day the community of Jesus knows what love is, God won't have any problem in pouring out His Spirit in power upon everybody. Alleluia!

So many of the issues that separate us are inconsequential, anyway. What do you believe on the millennium? Are you "pre-," "post-," or amillennial? That is all intellectual. What matters is, do you have the life of Jesus in you? Because the millennium is a secondary thing. If there is not going to be a millennium, it is not going to be, even if we all agree that it is going to be, and vice versa.

The main issue is the fruit of the life of the Spirit within you. Is the fruit of the Spirit millennium, rapture, vertical authority, demons and baptism? No! "The fruit of the Spirit is love, joy, peace, longsuffering, gentleness, goodness, faith, meekness and temperance" (Galatians 5:22, 23 KJV). The only way you can know the type of tree you are is by the fruit of your life, not by your doctrines.

If you have not the Spirit of Christ, you are not of Him. This is not to say that you should not believe in the millennium or a certain kind of baptism, but if you have not the Spirit of Christ, you are not of Him. Jesus came to give us life and love. It is the life you have that counts. Our doctrines are beautiful and nice, but they are nothing without love.

It seems to me that what we call doctrines are sometimes merely the traditions of our denominations. When I went to Bible school, I went to learn the Bible. But I was taught instead the doctrines of my denomination, and we used the Bible to prove them.

In a Presbyterian Bible school, you will read all the Calvinist verses. Go to a Seventh Day Adventist school and they prove from Scripture that the seventh day is the right day to worship. Then you go to a Pentecostal school and you learn that tongues are mentioned all through the pages of the Bible. You go to the Baptist seminary, and the Bible teaches you that tongues have ceased. Usually what we learn is our tradition, and we use the Bible to prove it.

We are so conditioned by our traditions that if we are truly to do God's will, He will have to open our heads, take out our brains, wash them in detergent, brush them and put them back in right-side up!

Another evidence of lack of growth is the issues we fight for. Children fight for anything. Sometimes when I serve Coca Cola to my children, it happens that one receives half an inch more than another one.

He says, "O Daddy, he has more Coca Cola than I do. Give me more."

"Daddy gave this to me!"

"O no! He has more Coke than me. Waaah!" They fight.

I say, "Another day I will give you more."

"No, I want more now!"

Then I give him some of mine. Why do I give it? Not because I am better, but just because I am grown up, and for me, peace is more important than half an inch of Coke. So also for us, the issues for which we fight tell us at what level we are.

One says, "If you receive the baptism in the Spirit, you must speak in tongues."

Another says, "I think I can receive it without speaking in tongues."

"No, no. That is not the Spirit."

Why not let him receive the Spirit anyway? God knows what to do. Do you think God doesn't know how to give the baptism in the Spirit?

A person was fighting with others about sanctification. They said sanctification is progressive. He said that sanctification is instantaneous, and that he was sanctified. That was good. No problem. But they argued so hard that this person who had sanctification lost it!

When we were in the world, we fought for politics or sports—the Giants or the Dodgers. Now we fight for doctrine. We have a holy fight.

It is like the couple who came to me and said, "Pastor, what a change since we got saved! We used to fight, my wife and I, with very bad words, and we even hit each other. But now, praise the Lord, no more bad words. We only fight with good words!"

Is it the same flesh in us expressing itself in "fighting for the faith" or for our rights that used to manifest itself in fighting for other things?

"No, I won't give up. Baptism has to be by immersion and that's all. If you do not accept this, you can leave."

How the Spirit of God grieves!

The doctrines we fight for tell us how we value things. Paul said that one eats everything, another eats vegetables only. One keeps one day, another counts all days alike. Please! Peace and love are more important than the day you keep or the food you eat! "For the kingdom of God is not eating and drinking, but righteousness and peace and joy in the Holy Spirit" (Romans 14:17 NASB). Some people will divide and destroy a community to save their point of view.

I don't say that we should not have convictions. Of course, we do. But I say that the issues we fight for tell the level of our spiritual growth. If we are fighting for the kingdom to come and His will to be done, and that we all come to love one another, no brother will be frightened off.

Issues! An issue is something we have to believe, apart from Jesus, in order to agree to be together. But anything in addition to Jesus, which we hold as essential for fellowship, is an idol. It may be Jesus plus tongues, Jesus plus a mode of baptism, Jesus plus discipleship, Jesus plus authority over demons—anything. However, Jesus Christ alone is enough to have communion. "Indeed our fellowship is with the Father, and with His Son Jesus Christ" (1 John 1:3 NASB).

Protestants have criticized the Catholics for making the way of salvation Jesus plus something else, but Protestants have their own Virgin Marys that have to help Jesus with salvation. Protestants do well when they say, "Come to Jesus!" But after the person comes, they spoil him when they start to teach him their doctrinal distinctions which divide the Body of Christ. "Be loyal to our church and to our denomination!" We have spoiled him.

Doctrines sometimes become idols. What? Yes, idols. You learn to be saved, then you must believe in Christ *and the millennium.* In order to be saved, you must believe in Christ *and in the Baptist church.* Then the Baptist church is an idol.

The Bible is as the star that led us to the manger, but we don't worship the star, nor the manger either. If we make of the means an end in itself, we become idolators.

Paul says, "If I speak with the tongues of men and of angels. . . . And if I have the gift of prophecy, and know all mysteries and all knowledge; and if I have all faith, so as to remove mountains, but do not have love, I am nothing" (1 Corinthians 13:1, 2 NASB). Look at all this—tongues of angels and men, prophecy, wisdom of God, mysteries, faith to move mountains, all this power without love is nothing. What then is the right way of performing baptism without love? Or any other activity of the church, without love? If all this power and wisdom of God is nothing without love, everything without love is equal to nothing. Nothing with love is equal to all. Alleluia!

If the love issue is less important to you than some of your doctrines, then that's up to you. For me, the love issue is most important. I have my convictions, but I have no problem with yours, because I love you. That's all. Love me and we won't have any problems in the kingdom of God. If I am wrong, perhaps your love is going to bring me to the cross. If you are wrong and I keep loving, perhaps some light will shine on you. But let's love one another.

THE FRUIT OF THE SPIRIT

Gal. 5:22,23

Music by
JUAN CARLOS ORTIZ

The fruit of the Spir - it is love, love, joy, peace, long suf - f'ring, gen - tle - ness, good - ness, faith, meek - ness, tem - p'rance and love, a - gainst which there is no law.

Love, joy, peace, long suf - f'ring, gen - tle - ness, good - ness, faith, meek - ness, tem - p'rance and love.

5

Cry of the Human Heart

Perhaps you have a problem with me now. I said that spiritual maturity is the answer to most of these problems wracking the Church today — spiritual maturity which gives a person God's perspective, God's love and all the other good fruits of the Spirit. But many churches go on for decades and many Christians live all their lives without reaching this spiritual maturity. How do we get spiritual maturity?

I want to point out some spiritual facts of life. Let's look at some of the obvious stages a person goes through when he begins the Christian life.

After we make that journey from the kingdom of darkness to the kingdom of light, it is wonderful. How happy we are in this beautiful new kingdom! We have joy, we have peace, we have love. Everything is different. For awhile. Then little by little, we come back to earth. The peace and the joy are not there so much. Some of the old problems we thought had gone away only went into hiding temporarily. Now they come back. Spiritually we go up and down.

But it may help to know that this on-again, off-again spiritual experience is not unique to us. Millions of Christians have made this very same journey, including a famous man of God many centuries ago. This famous man was King David. Listen as he describes his experience.

> For I know my transgressions,
> And my sin is ever before me.
> Against Thee, Thee only, have I sinned,
> And done what is evil in Thy sight,
> So that Thou art justified when Thou dost speak,
> And blameless when Thou dost judge.
>
> Behold, I was brought forth in iniquity,
> And in sin did my mother conceive me.
> Behold, Thou dost desire truth in the innermost
>   being,
> And in the hidden part Thou wilt make me know
>   wisdom.
> Purify me with hyssop, and I shall be clean;
> Wash me, and I shall be whiter than snow.
> Make me to hear joy and gladness,
> Let the bones which Thou hast broken rejoice.
> Hide Thy face from my sins,
> And blot out all my iniquities.
>
> Create in me a clean heart, O God,
> And renew a steadfast spirit within me.
>   Psalm 51:3-10 NASB

This is the cry of David's heart. David was a man who really, really wanted to please God. If there was a man in the Old Testament who loved and respected God, it was David. He was a man according to the heart of God. David had talks with God. He knew God. He had God in the first place in his life. Nevertheless he failed deeply. He committed adultery and was responsible for another man's death.

I suppose David examined himself: *Am I not a man who wants to please God? Do I not pray? Do I not make the best psalms to God? Do I not feel God's presence? Do I not talk with God? Is not God first in my life? Then how could it be that I fell into this sin? How could I fail so deeply?*

After his examination of his motives and his love for God, he found everything was right. His respect for the law was perfect. His desire to please God was O.K. His order of priorities was God first. So, what had happened?

How can a person that is willing to please God, to do His will, to have God's laws in first place, fall into sin? . . . And what a sin!

David's cry embodies the cry of the whole of mankind. The cry of you and me. It is the cry of each man and woman who wants to please God, wants to do His will, but nevertheless fails, grieves God and becomes separated from Him.

This is really what it means to be spiritually thirsty. Thirst is not just an abstract emptiness within us. Thirst is that frustration and depression when we cannot live up to God's standards as they were recorded. We can't! That perfect will of God, that holiness, that purity, that love we have heard about, where is it?

Thirst is that desire to have a clean conscience, to be inwardly tranquil, to live without any condemnation. What a problem! To be willing and not to be able to accomplish! That is the greatest struggle we face within us.

God knows all about it. He said in Noah's day that every intent of the thoughts of man's heart was only evil continually (Genesis 6:5).

Paul said, "I am of flesh, sold into bondage to sin" (Romans 7:14 KJV). Sold to sin! He also said he knew nothing good dwelt in him (Romans 7:18); that man is hostile toward God and cannot subject himself to His law (Romans 8:7).

David said, "Behold, I was brought forth in iniquity, and in sin my mother conceived me" (Psalm 51:5). That is the problem. Any person who by his own strength tries to live a life of perfection and holiness will discover with sadness that it is impossible for him.

David made this discovery and then said something very wise: "Create in me a clean heart, O God, and renew a steadfast spirit within me."

In other words, David came to understand the incapacity of man to meet God's requirements. His heart was the problem, not God's laws. He didn't beg, "Please, God, give us easier laws, please!" No, he didn't. He said, "God, create in me a clean heart, and unless you create in me a clean heart, I won't be able to please You, O God."

It was even worse with Adam and Eve. Some people say, "If Adam and Eve hadn't fallen, we would be living a happy life in the Garden of Eden." Not so. They were innocent when they fell, but innocence is no guarantee. If they hadn't sinned, their children would have, or you and I would have!

Paul said, after his self-examination, "Wretched man that I am! Who will set me free from the body of this death" (Romans 7:24 KJV)?

This is the cry of mankind — your cry.

Man was created for God, but there is a tremendous struggle, a continual tension: heaven and hell, the spirit and the flesh. And that brings a continual thirst in our souls.

David wrote a song about it.

O how I love Thy law!
It is my meditation all the day.
Thy commandments make me wiser than my
    enemies. . . .
I have more insight than my teachers,
For Thy testimonies are my meditation,
I understand more than the aged,
Because I have observed Thy precepts.
I have restrained my feet from every evil way,
That I may keep Thy word.
I have not turned aside from Thine ordinances,
For Thou Thyself hast taught me.
How sweet are Thy words to my taste!
Yes, sweeter than honey to my mouth!
From Thy precepts I get understanding;
Therefore I hate every false way.

                       Psalm 119:97-104 NASB

You know that King David lived under what we call the Law. He read the laws and then tried to obey them. So we can define this type of religion as a system based on obedience to written commandments.

David was one of the best religious men in the Old Testament. And his was the right religion, the best in the Old World. He had the religion, but not the new covenant life. He had a religion of precepts, concepts and principles. That was the problem even though he was very zealous.

He had the true God and he had a holy book. He had to

obey the things written in the book. He rightly called the holy book the Word of God. He read in the book and tried to obey it. That was very much like the religion of some of us, and surprisingly like every other religion.

Nearly every religion has a holy book, and people try to live according to the book. Muslims try to live according to the Koran, Buddhists according to Buddha's thoughts, and Christians according to the Bible. Sometimes I do not see too much difference between *our* usual practice and other people's religions.

David had that type of religion. It was a pattern of life based on obedience to a book. But how can you obey a holy book with a crooked heart? The book is good, but the heart is evil.

Unless a work of grace is done, a religious system creates problems, besides not giving a solution for man's situation.

Sometimes we get some success. We get success in not smoking, not drinking and some other things. But this is only a religious system. When we have some success, that success is in the flesh. It is out of our own effort. It is called in the Scriptures "works of the flesh," or "dead works," be-cause it is performed by the flesh and not by the Spirit. And that creates pride.

"I don't drink! I don't smoke! I don't do that — Ahem!" Just like the Pharisees. You feel nice. Be careful when you feel nice in yourself.

But of course, if we fail and nobody notices it, we still look like we are holy. So we become hypocrites. David fell and nobody knew it, so he kept on as if he were having fun in sin. He went to the temple singing the Scriptures. Hypo-crite! We have lots of that in the Church. The young people who sing in the choir, nobody knows what they are, so they sing in the choir. The deacon and even the pastor are the same. This system of life based in obedience to written com-mandments obliges us to be hypocrites.

Don't fool yourself, we preachers know in our own experience that by our own effort we cannot do God's will.
We don't like to be hypocrites, because of our church doctrine. I cannot come from the pulpit and say, "Dear
brothers, today I was speaking against that other
preacher. I thought that I could speak much better than he
on that passage." No, we don't say that. We just have it in
our hearts. Nobody knows. But God knows. That's the
nature of man, he is wicked. And there are many other sins
we do not tell. We are hypocrites.

To appear that we are holy, we point out other people's
sins. That lady is painting her lips, so we look scandalized.
Then there is judgment in the church.

Do you remember the time Nathan came to David?
Nathan told a story of a rich man who needed a lamb to
cook for a visitor. Instead of taking one of his own many
lambs, he seized the only lamb of a poor man. It was a
lamb that the family loved as a person, who slept with the
man as a son.

And King David said, "That rich man has to die!" How
quick you are to judge others, David! He was one of us, because in judging others we want to appear holy and right-
eous.

But Nathan turned it around and said, "David, you are
the rich man who did this!"

When we have been discovered, we, too, feel condemned.
Depressed. How many ups and downs there are in our
religious lives. David had them. One day he sings, "I will
destroy my enemies!" Another day, he sobs, "Have mercy
on me, O Lord." Ups and downs mean that we are living
after a system of religion based on obedience to written
commandments. This system creates in the Church pride,
hypocrisy, judgment and depression.

It also creates laws that don't exist in the Bible. Because
it has no life, everything has to be ruled by laws. If I have

joy, I have joy. But if I have no joy, we have to put a law there: "Rejoice in the Lord." Everything becomes a law. We have that. The Jews have that: the traditions, the Talmud. There was a law among the Jews that they should not eat an egg that a hen laid on a Saturday!

We also have laws. Thou shalt not smoke. Thou shalt close thine eyes to pray. Thou shalt not read newspapers on Sunday. In the church in which I grew up, we couldn't play football. We couldn't wear a swimming suit and swim in the swimming pool. Thou shalt not paint thine lips. Thou shalt not wear a wig. Many, many rules. It is endless, according to the denomination you belong to.

In Germany, they don't paint their lips, but they drink beer. In the U.S., they don't drink beer, but they paint from eyes to toes. Biblical legalism confuses us into the legalism of traditions, even of cultural things.

In my country, the biggest Protestant church is the Plymouth Brethren. The English people came to Argentina to make a railway system. So they brought the Plymouth Brethren Gospel. The Argentines drink "maté," a green, herb tea. When the English came, those who got converted started to drink English tea at four o'clock in the afternoon. We thought their tea was more evangelical than maté! We made tea a law.

What is legalism? Listen. It is a system of life based on obedience to laws. That is the type of life David lived. It is the type of life everybody lives. Don't touch! Go to bed! Don't go out! Be careful! All day long. Then we go to school, we go to church. Don't do! Laws! Laws!

We need a new heart. That's what David cried for. This system of laws didn't bring any solution to the cry of man. The Law worsened the problem. The Law didn't satisfy the thirst of the soul. David and Israel are examples. Under the Law a person cannot please God. Law is a life of ups and downs. The Law fools us. It tempts us to fulfill it.

We go to a tent meeting. There are people who get consecrated in every camp meeting. They live from camp meeting to camp meeting, from revival to revival. That is not God's will.

The cry of David is relevant: "Create in me a clean heart, O Lord; and renew a right spirit within me!" Then comes the great promise of the Father.

6

The New Heart

"Behold, days are coming," declares the Lord, "when I will make a a new covenant with the house of Israel and with the house of Judah, not like the covenant which I made with their fathers, in the day I took them by the hand to bring them out of the land of Egypt, My covenant which they broke, although I was a husband to them," declares the Lord.

"But this is the covenant which I will make with the house of Israel after those days," declares the Lord, "I will put My law within them, and on their heart I will write it; and I will be their God, and they shall be My people.

"And they shall not teach again, each man his neighbor and each man his brother, saying, 'Know the Lord,' for they shall all know Me, from the least of them to the greatest of them," declares the Lord, "for I will forgive their iniquity, and their sin I will remember no more."

Jeremiah 31:31-34 NASB

Alleluia! A new covenant! I want to underline the word *new*. Some people think that the new covenant is a reformation of the old covenant — instead of the Saturday Sabbath, they had Sunday, and some other changes making a new set of laws. No, it is not an adaptation of the old law into the living situation of today. It is completely new.

The first thing God said about the new covenant was that the new one was not going to be like the former one—the covenant of Mt. Sinai. That was a system of religion based on obedience to written commandments. It won't be like that, said God. It is not changing hard laws for easier laws—nothing like that.

Some people think that the old covenant is the Ten Commandments and the new covenant is the Sermon on the Mount. No, the Sermon on the Mount is just the interpretation by the Writer of the old commandments. Jesus was saying to His people, "The Lord says, 'Thou shalt not commit adultery,' but I am the Maker of the Law, and I will explain to you what that law really means. What My Father and I had in mind when We said that was even if you look at another woman ... but of course, without a new heart you couldn't do that commandment, so We just said, 'Don't commit adultery;' We couldn't go any farther than that." The Sermon on the Mount is not a new code of ethics, it is a spiritual interpretation of the Law, the real spirit that was behind it.

Why should there be a new covenant? Because Israel broke the old covenant, although God was a husband to them. The Lord says there had to be a new covenant because nobody can accomplish the old covenant, nobody can keep the law of God. Nobody can.

And so God said, "I will put My law within them, and on their heart will I write it." Where did God say He was going to put His laws? In another book—one with India paper and a black cover? No! "On their *heart* I will write it." He promises to put His desires within us. The India paper book is just a poor copy of what God writes in our hearts. There is no problem with the Book. The Book is good. Other religions are founded on a book, even the Christian religion, though the Bible is absolutely unique among them. But only those who have God's mind inside are the sons of God.

"I will be their God," promised the Lord. I Myself in Person will be their God, not a set of doctrines, not a book. In Person, I will abide in them and will walk in them. They shall be My people and I will be their God. This is the restoration of a right relationship with God.

Then He said, nobody will have to teach his neighbor or his brother who He is or how He acts because everybody will have Him inside.

The main difference between the old covenant and the new covenant is that the old is a commandment from outside, the new is an urge from inside. There is the Law plainly written on the stone: Don't do this! Do that! . . . *All right, I'll try. . . . Oh, it's hard! I'll wait and see if it is any easier tomorrow. . . . Ah, it's just the same!* The Ten Commandments were engraved on static stone. But the new covenant is a dynamic urge, from inside to out. These are the rivers of living water Jesus was talking about.

In my country girls used to be very helpful around the house. But nowadays they take too much care of their nails and hands, so they don't like to do dishes or wash the floors, and mother has to do all those things. Or the girls do it, but with complaining and wailing, "Oooh, I'll ruin my hands!"

But the day comes when the girl is to introduce a very special boy to the house. She gets up early in the morning. Singing tra-la-la-la-la-la, she starts to clean and polish everything. She has an urge from inside. Ah, it's love! The boyfriend is coming and she wants to make the house very clean. "Mama, is there something else I can do?" She doesn't feel tired, it's easy.

"What has happened today?" asks Mama.

"I don't know, Mom. I just have an urge from inside to be clean."

That is the way God wants us to serve Him. When you do things to fulfill commandments, it spoils your relationship with God and violates love.

Suppose I get married and I have no love for my wife, so I buy a book, *How a Husband Has to Behave.* I say, "Let's see what the book says." It says to give your wife a kiss every morning. So in the morning I say, "Hello, Martha, are you ready for the morning kiss? . . . There! I have finished with that commandment. I can check it off."

And Martha says, "Listen, Johnny, do you kiss me to obey a law, or because you feel something inside that makes you want to?"

"Oh, no, I don't feel anything, I just want to be obedient in order to go to heaven."

"Then, Johnny, I don't want it."

When we do things from law, it spoils the relationship. It has to come from the heart or it is of no avail, it is unclean. If we are obeying commandments in order to go to heaven, we are saying that God has to pay us for the effort. God has to give me something because I was a good boy. That is a forced relationship.

Ezekiel 36: 26, 27 adds something important: "Moreover, I will give you a new heart and put a new spirit within you; and I will remove the heart of stone from your flesh and give you a heart of flesh. And I will put My Spirit

within you and cause you to walk in My statutes . . ."
(NASB)

It is not a new code of ethics He is giving us. It is the answer to the cry of the human heart, "Create in me a clean heart, O God, and renew a right spirit within me." God answers that He will give a new heart and He will put His Spirit within us. This is tremendous! The law is good and just, we don't have to change the law. It is the heart that needs to be changed.

If you are driving on the highway and the engine blows up, you won't fix the car by changing a tire. You have to change the motor! Even if God could have changed some laws, man would still be condemned. I think that the written law of God is still too soft. I think that God's real requirements are much more than what the Old Testament says. You can see that by the Sermon on the Mount.

The old covenant is the letter of commandments outside us, the new covenant is a new heart and His Spirit within.

The new heart is a very modern heart with everything built in. God made it in the laboratory of heaven—a tender heart, because man had a stony heart before. The law was on a stone so you can imagine a stone hitting a stone—just sparks! But God has made a soft heart with His laws built in. In Jeremiah God said, "I will put my law within them, and on their heart I will write it." They will have My mind in them, My thoughts for every situation, so that in every circumstance they will know what to do and what not to do. Alleluia! That's what the Bible says.

"And I will put My Spirit within you and cause you to walk in My statutes." Who is going to cause us to walk? He will cause us to walk in His ways, and to keep His ordinances and do them. That's the only way. That is grace. God does everything. What the law could not do, God did (Romans 8:3). That is the promise of the Father.

It is a heart with everything built in—all God's desires

are built in, all His laws are built in. Now it is not a book, but the Author of the book inside. It is tremendous—very different from the old covenant.

The law was: "Read this and try to do it!" Now it is, "I will put My Spirit within you, and from within you I will cause you to walk in My statutes." That's the only hope. Because if He doesn't, well . . . the holiest men we read about in the Bible, David and Paul, they couldn't, even though they loved the Law.

"I will cause you to walk in my statutes."

"Me?"

"Yes, you."

"Impossible!"

"Yes, possible."

"I can't."

"*I* can."

"But I am weak."

"But *I* am strong. *I* will cause you to walk, Johnny."

"O Lord! As You know, I try, but . . ."

"Who says try again? I will put My Spirit within you, and I will cause you to walk in My statutes."

Tremendous, isn't it? This is the new covenant.

Some people think that the old covenant is the Old Testament, and the new covenant is the New Testament. That's wrong. Old covenant is letter, new covenant is Spirit and life. Even the New Testament can be taken in the old covenant fashion. We can read the New Testament in the old covenant way. We can make it a system of religion based on obedience to written commandments.

But the new pact has to be within us. That is really the difference. It is the new heart with God's Spirit within us causing us to walk in Him and answering the cry of David and the thirst of the soul. New covenant is a life that flows from the Spirit. Alleluia!

New covenant is not to have new writings, but the

Author of the writings within. That is God's promise in the Scriptures. How did David know to cry out for a clean heart and a right spirit within him? I am really amazed at this. But David was an expert in divine relationships.

Old covenant is to be led by outward rules. New covenant is to be led by the urge of the Spirit within us. It's a completely different thing. Old covenant is Romans chapter seven. It is a life of struggling: I want to, but I can't. I try to, then I say, "Lord, forgive me because I couldn't, but I'll start over again tomorrow and try again."

So we start the first of January. "Lord, now we are going to do Thy will." We go to the fifth of January and then we fall again. We say, "God, please have mercy!" Ups and downs and ups and downs. That is Romans chapter seven, and it finishes, "O wretched man that I am, who shall deliver me from the body of this death."

But the new covenant is pictured in Romans chapter eight. The law of the Spirit of life in Jesus Christ has made me free from the law of sin that was in me . . . There is no condemnation for those who walk after the Spirit.

The letter requires holiness, but the Spirit imparts holiness. The letter asks something that we cannot give. We say in Spanish, "Don't ask figs from a pear tree." Don't ask holiness from a stony heart. The letter requires. The Spirit imparts. The letter says, "Thou shalt not be bald!" But the Spirit says, "Receive the hair!" Poor man under the law. He has to say, "I'm sorry, but I can't help being bald."

At this point, we should start asking ourselves: "Under which covenant am I living?"

You have the New Testament, but the New Testament is not a code of rules. It is just a picture of those who lived in the Spirit. It tells us how it is to have life in the Spirit. In the primitive Church, the best days of the Church, they didn't have the New Testament written yet. Notice that they had more power, more life and more guidance before they had the New Testament!

Why are there so many people in the Church still living under condemnation—up and down, up and down? Because they still have a type of religion which is based on obedience to written commandments. If they have the new heart, they are not using it. This can happen.

I lived in the country where we had to pump the water. Pumping water is hard work. One day the running water came. Just open the faucet . . . a sound like shhhhhhh . . . and the water ran! But some people loved the old system, so they kept on pumping. They were not using the running water, even though they had it! Don't be like that.

The promise of the Father is life, joy and peace. The whole Old Testament is full of this promise. Look at Isaiah 35:8. "And a highway shall be there, and a way, and it shall be called the way of holiness; the unclean shall not pass over it; but it shall be for those: the wayfaring men, though fools, shall not err therein." (KJV). It shall be for those who walk that way, and fools will not wander on it. Look at this new way of holiness: even the most foolish won't wander on it. Better a fool with a new heart than a wise person with an old heart. Don't worry, you won't err if you are walking after the Spirit. You walk where the Spirit leads. This is God's solution to the cry of the human heart.

7

The Unveiled Christ

God's gift of life to us came in a special wrapping. When Jesus walked on earth, His flesh was a veil, or wrapping, around that gift.

Jesus' death on the cross not only atoned for our sins, but did away with His flesh, in order to reveal His Spirit, the eternal Lord. On the cross the wrapping paper came off. On the day of Pentecost the Spirit of Jesus came to be in us, "the promise of the Father." The Spirit of God came to be inside of every human being who receives Him.

The letter of the Old Testament was a veil in front of Jesus Christ. That letter was done away when He was revealed. Behind the letter was the reality. When we go to a play, we first see the play's title on the poster out in front. But when they take the curtain away, we begin to see the play itself. The letter just says, "It's coming! It's going to be. Wait!"

But we can keep Jesus behind the curtain, or wrapping, just as someone might keep a gift wrapped up because the paper and ribbon are nice. If we are too conscious of the letter and do not look behind it, we may miss the real Person and be worshippers of the veil, the curtain.

The Word made flesh is not the end. Even in Jesus Christ, walking this earth, something was still veiled. The writer to the Hebrews says that we have boldness to enter into the holiest through the veil, that is to say, His body (Hebrews 10:20). So also the flesh was a veil. Actually, the gift package was double-wrapped.

First, Jesus said, "The Law said this . . ., But I say . . .; because I am the Maker of the Law and greater than the letter." Saying this, He removed one wrapper.

Then, He said, "It is expedient for you that I go away" (John 16:7 KJV). Another wrapper was going to be taken away.

What will you do? Will you worship the wrapping paper? The real thing was still inside — the promise of the Father, "I will give you after those days a new heart. I will put My Spirit within you, and I will cause you to walk in My statutes" (Ezekiel 36:26, 27). That is the real thing.

God's people waited a long time for their Messiah. When Jesus came, the disciples thought that now everything was accomplished. Here we have the King. Here we have the One of whom the Scriptures spoke. Alleluia!

The disciples ask, "Is this the time for the kingdom?"

"Not yet. I have to go away. This body must disappear that you may have the real thing that was promised, that is the Spirit within you that will cause you to walk in God's statutes."

Those thirty-three years of Jesus' life are precious and wonderful. Nevertheless, we have to proceed in the revelation of God's purposes. When I went to Bible school, we had a subject called The Life of Christ. It covered only from the manger to the ascension. That's not the life of Christ! That's just thirty-three years, and in one way it is the poorest picture of Jesus. It was the picture of the Jesus who was made of no reputation, the picture of Him as He took the form of a servant, the picture of the Jesus that came in the image of man.

And I have to confess that all my life I was told only about the Jesus in the flesh. When I was a boy, we started with the manger and we studied the twelve-year-old boy, the baptism, the temptations, the miracles and parables, the death on the cross and the resurrection; then back to the manger! That is the reason why we don't grow, because all our knowledge of Jesus centers in the Jesus after the flesh.

Paul said, "Henceforth we know no man after the flesh. And even though we knew Jesus after the flesh, we don't know Him any more that way" (2 Corinthians 5:16). Too much consciousness of Jesus after the flesh is a hindrance in knowing Jesus, the eternal Lord, who was behind the flesh.

The same thing can be said of the letter. Too much consciousness of the letter, gives the letter the wrong place, so that the letter becomes an end in itself rather than a pointing finger to the real thing.

We find a sign that says: "Oregon, 200 miles." That sign is supposed to help us get to Oregon, but it is going to be a hindrance if we say, "Oh, wonderful! See, it's Oregon! Let's put our camper here."

But that's not Oregon. It is just a sign saying that to get to Oregon you have to keep on going. If you stay there, the sign that was supposed to help you becomes a hindrance. Even so, we can become letter-centered.

The letter points to Jesus. Jesus in the flesh was part of

the promise, but the final fulfillment was that the Holy Spirit of the living God, the Spirit of Jesus, would dwell in each one of us and cause us to walk in God's ways.

The Corinthian church quarreled much about its leadership. After Paul had introduced the Way there, Apollos came to preach, and then Peter came. And of course Apollos was mightily used of God, so people loved him. He was a much better preacher than Paul, so perhaps the young people went after Apollos. Maybe it was the old people who said, "No, Paul was a better man of God."

Then Peter came. Peter was different from Paul and different from Apollos. He had something distinctive — he had been with Jesus, walked with Him, ate with Him, slept with Him. He electrified the audience when he spoke.

Maybe the announcement before Peter's coming was: "Now we are going to have a visit from one of the Twelve! We have never had that experience before, dear brethren. Peter is one who lived with Jesus!"

So the whole crowd came, and Peter may have started by saying, "Dear brothers and sisters, as you know, I was one of the Twelve, and I say with modesty, I was one of the closest three. I had the privilege to see with these two eyes everything that Jesus did.

"I remember once we were walking down the street, and Jesus said to me (remember we were very close friends), He said to me, 'Peter, I feel hungry.' You can imagine how I felt! I said to Him, 'Nobody has anything. I'm sorry we have nothing to give you, but look, Lord, here is a fig tree.' I knew that He loved figs. 'Oh,' He said, 'let's go see if we can find some figs.' And I almost wept when I saw there was not one fig for our Lord.

"But do you know what happened? O brothers, I am a personal witness to it! I was there! Look, my skin gets goosebumps when I think of it! He said to the fig tree, 'Fig tree, nobody will eat any more fruit from you!' And you know what happened? Brother, I've seen it, I've seen it! The fig tree started to dry up!"

Peter was stealing the hearts of the people from Paul. No wonder the people said afterwards, "Paul is not an apostle. He didn't see the Lord." So Paul writes to the Corinthians, "From now on we recognize no man according to the flesh." Perhaps that was for Peter. "Even though we have known Christ according to the flesh, yet now we know Him thus no longer" (2 Corinthians 5:16 NASB).

What does he mean? In a way he is saying that he is glad he did not see Jesus after the flesh. He had something less to unlearn. He had one problem less. Problem? Not that knowing Jesus in the flesh is a problem. Please don't misunderstand me. But to be more conscious of His earthly life than of the eternal Lord Himself is dangerous. We tend to be static, you know, not dynamic and growing in the knowledge of the Lord. If we know Him with a beard, forever we imagine Him with a beard. Perhaps He got shaved after that!

To know only the historic Christ is a retrospective and static knowledge. To know Him as He is now is a dynamic and growing knowledge.

When we see some new facet of truth, we make an institution of that new light. We write a book, for example, on "discipleship" or "submission," and then make an institution out of it! That is letter.

So Paul says he has one problem less. If he had known Christ in the flesh, he would try to erase that image from his mind and heart. Why? In order to give place to the unveiled Lord, the Spirit, the new covenant, the promise of the Father. That flesh of Jesus has to fade away.

You know how Paul knew Jesus for the first time. He never saw the Jesus of sandals and beard. The first time he had contact with Jesus, he almost died. Jesus was up in heaven and Paul was going to Damascus.

And Jesus said, "Oh, that man is going to Damascus. I will say something to him." So He opened the window of heaven, and Jesus was a little bit careless. He let so much of His glory shine through that window that it almost killed Paul. Jesus shut the window quickly, but Paul fell to the ground and was blind for three days!

Then Paul encountered Jesus again when he was taken up to the third heaven. Paul saw Christ in His central office on the third floor of God's building. Ah! Didn't Paul know Jesus? Paul didn't know the veiled Jesus; he knew the unveiled Christ, the inward, the eternal Lord with the glory He had from the beginning before the ages.

I don't know how you imagine heaven. Even though I am a Pentecostal, I used to imagine heaven as an Episcopalian procession. There was Jesus with a crown and rod of gold, and the seraphs and the cherubs and all the angels on both sides, and we would all be in the holy procession. I don't know why I thought like that.

But since I became better acquainted with the living Lord, I understand that my imagination of the Episcopalian heaven came through my interpretation of the letter. The book of Revelation described some big meetings in heaven, and I imagined that heaven is always like that. Now I have discovered that heaven is more friendly and warm than processions. Now I think of Jesus living there.

Can't you hear Him? "O Michael, how are you? Nice to see you. How is your family?"

I think heaven is more friendship than processions, and I think they have some jokes too! Maybe an angel would tell one like this.

"Come here, friends, let me tell you. Last evening I was in earth and they were having this meeting, and it was funny. A preacher was trying to tell how tremendous the power of Christ is and he used the example of Jesus cursing the fig tree! Can you imagine? Christ created the galaxies, and he tells about the fig tree! Ha ha, ho ho!"

And Jesus speaks up, "Don't laugh. When I cursed the fig tree, it was when I was made of no reputation. I took the form of a servant and I was in the likeness of man. In that condition cursing a fig tree was something to remember. You don't know because you have not been down there in the flesh as I was. You were created angels. You are flying from galaxy to galaxy in seconds. You really do not understand what it is to be in the body of flesh. There you cannot walk much more than three miles an hour. You know nothing about that, but I know. In that situation it is tremendous to curse the fig tree."

Well, which Jesus do you know? The body of Jesus was the veil of the Spirit. This is something like the tabernacle, with its outer court, the holy place and the holiest. When you get to the outer court, you think you have everything. Praise the Lord! You enter with joy, but then you find out there is the holy place. When you get in there, again you think you have everything. But yet there is the holiest place.

I don't think the Lord meant that we should be forty years in the outer court and forty years in the holy place. Because the veil was torn, we can go right into the holiest by the blood of Jesus. I think that more and more of those who are converted are going to be born according to the new covenant. They won't need to live for years hung up on the letter.

We understand that the Gentiles do not need to go first through the Law and then become followers of Jesus. But you remember that most of the early believers thought that the Gentiles first had to be circumcised and keep the Law of Moses, to become Jews, and then become Christians. Paul understood that Gentiles could be "called out" ones right away without going through the Law.

I think that very soon the new converts are going to be

born in a cradle in the holiest place — in the Spirit and not after the letter. Now we are in the dispensation of no veils. It is a new dispensation! The unveiled Spirit of God is in us.

Of course, this has many implications. Paul speaks of "God, whom I serve in my spirit" (Romans 1:9 NASB). Jesus said that true worship is the worship in the spirit (John 4:24). There is physical worship, soulish worship, and a spirit worship that is deeper than the other two types of worship.

There is physical worship where only the presence of the body in the pew and the kneeling are taken as important. It is an advantage to come into soul worship where we do it with feeling. We really mean it. We put all our mind and thought into it. That is a good meeting. Nevertheless, if we go no farther than that, it could be another hindrance.

When we learn to worship in the Spirit, we are no longer controlled by our circumstances. When Paul writes about serving the Lord in the Spirit, he means we don't need any organ or candles or instruction — nothing. I could sit in a tavern and have the closest fellowship with God with all that carousing going on around me, because my worship is in the Spirit.

Do not depend on atmosphere. When we need atmosphere, that's soulish. Of course, when you learn to worship Him in Spirit, you can put your soul and your body and everything into worship. But if you have learned how to worship Him in the Spirit, where those innermost parts are in communion with God, you don't need any emotion. The service of God in the Spirit is not emotional, it is spiritual. Spiritual is deeper than emotional and more serious. Sometimes you may have a tremendous revelation of the Spirit without touching your emotions.

Some people cannot have a good meeting if they do not have a deep silence or a lot of noise.

One says, "Oh, I couldn't worship today."

"What happened?"

"I had a toothache."

Or, "I didn't feel very well and couldn't enjoy the meeting."

If you had been with Paul and Silas in the jail, with a bleeding back, would you have enjoyed the meeting? I have learned that life in the Spirit is much deeper than the circumstances around me.

Why all this teaching about the Law? If we were Jewish people, born under the letter, it would be more justified. My concern is that we, who were born nearly two thousand years after Jesus tore the veil are still living under the law! Of course, Jewish people are under the Law of the Old Testament, and we are under the law of the New Testament, but under law nevertheless.

Do you know what has happened with the life in the Spirit? It was very clearly revealed to the primitive believers. But it suffered almost the same fate as the Book of the Law in the days of Josiah. You remember that the book was lost. Nobody knew about it. One day they were cleaning the temple and somebody found a book.

"What's this? — Thou shalt not commit adultery — it sounds religious. I will take it to one of the priests." The priest took it to the king.

King Josiah said, "Oooh! the laws we have not kept! We didn't know that it was here! How could such a thing happen in Israel?"

So the king set everybody to fasting according to the Law and to turning to God again. You remember this from 2 Chronicles 34.

The same thing has happened with the Spirit in our churches. We have been trying to clean up the Church a bit and have found something. "What's this? It is something we have seldom seen!" Now we can see that this life in the

Spirit was the way of life of the primitive Church. Living this way made them write the epistles. Under the letter, they were slaves of the letter. Under the Spirit, they were makers of the letter. They were Spirit-minded. Jesus was unveiled to them. He is for us, too.

8

The New Husband

The Law was our husband. We were bound to the Law. We had to do the will of the Law and it had a very big belt-strap for spankings when we failed. Poor people under the law!

For the married woman is bound by the law to her husband while he is living; but if her husband dies, she is released from the law concerning her husband.

So then if, while her husband is living, she is joined to another man, she shall be called an adulteress; but if her husband dies, she is free from the law, so that she is not an adulteress, though she is joined to another man.

Therefore, my brethren, you also were made to die to the Law through the body of Christ, that you might be joined to another, to Him who was raised from the dead, that we might bear fruit for God.

For while we were in the flesh, the sinful passions which were aroused by the Law, were at work in the members of our body to bear fruit for death.

But now we have been released from the Law, having died to that by which we were bound, so that we serve in newness of the Spirit and not in oldness of the letter.

Romans 7: 2-6 NASB.

Jesus loved us. He saw our condition, married to the Law. The only way to be free of that Law was by death, and so He provided a death for us. He died for us.

I was born again to belong to another husband: Jesus Christ within me. He now is my Husband. He doesn't spank me. He enables me to walk in His ways.

Now here is a problem. For years and years the people in my church and I were living an adulterous relationship with two husbands!

I will tell you my experience. I don't want you to think I am pointing at you. I tried to fulfill the letter, the written commandment, with all my heart. I tried to be on good terms with my old husband.

I said, "I'll fulfill this commandment, Lord." Then when I failed, I went to the new Husband.

"O Lord, forgive me, I have failed. I know that You died for me, and that Thy blood is enough. Cleanse me with that blood! Won't You forgive me?"

And the Lord would say, "Yes, I forgive you. That's My grace."

"Thank you! Now I am in victory again and can fulfill

the written commandments and be faithful to the former husband."

I tried to, and when I fell, I once again went to the second Husband.

"Praise God! He forgave me! He had mercy on me! Oh, the blood of Jesus! I have confessed my sin, O Alleluia, God forgave me!"

Then right back to trying to fulfill the written commandments. From camp meeting to camp meeting, making consecrations, receiving the pardon of God, and then going back to the other husband. You know what this is called? Adultery. It is to live with two husbands, using Jesus' services to fix our problems with the former husband, His rival.

It was not so long ago that I learned to live for only one Husband, Jesus Christ. There is no more condemnation. I live guided by the Spirit. My former problems ended.

I was writing my notes for a videotape session at two in the morning recently. I put something down. The Spirit said, "No." So I didn't say that. No problem. It's interesting to live this life. He is showing me how to walk.

I trust Him. I live with Him, for Him. I have no more problems. Even if I miss the pathway somewhere, He will take care of it. I am truly convinced that this wonderful life of the new covenant is based, not on written commandments, but on quick response to the life of the Spirit within me.

Don't you see the picture? Paul says, "But now we have been released from the Law, having died to that by which we were bound, so that we serve in newness of the Spirit and not in oldness of the letter" (Romans 7:6 NASB).

Law and grace, letter and Spirit, are things completely different — like heaven and earth. It was a shock for me when I realized this. I received this message during one of those weeks when I get alone with the Lord in fasting and prayer. I usually take a whole epistle on a cassette.

That week I read aloud the epistle to the Romans; then I heard it on tape. When I finished, I started again and I meditated and prayed. When I had the whole epistle in my mind — the whole, not just pieces — I knew that I had been missing everything in that epistle. Everything? Yes. Because I always took that epistle as the letter, something good, but I never understood the real thing to which the letter pointed. I had found a sign pointing to Oregon and made the sign an end to itself and never got to Oregon!

Then I saw that Law is letter, grace is Spirit and life. I wound up confessing spiritual adultery with two husbands. You will notice in Romans that Paul uses "to be under the law" and "to be under the flesh" in the same way. They are interchangeable. Part of the problem is that the flesh needs a law, and she makes it.

"However you are not in the flesh but in the Spirit, if indeed the Spirit of God dwells in you. But if anyone does not have the Spirit of Christ, he does not belong to Him" (Romans 8:9 NASB).

"But I have the Bible!"

"That's good, but it's not enough," He says. "The Spirit of Christ is the Agent in the new covenant. Christ in you is the hope of glory."

"Ah."

"For if ye live after the flesh, ye shall die: but if through the reading of the New Testament ye do mortify the deeds of the body, ye shall live." Is that so? No. What does it really say?

"If ye through the Spirit do mortify the deeds of the body ... " Through what? Through the Spirit. This is the new covenant.

I was the teacher of Romans in our seminary, and I never saw this. I had a mixture of law and grace. I was teaching verse by verse, but I never understood this. Look!

"For all who are being led by the Spirit of God, these are sons of God" (Romans 8:14 NASB). Who are the sons of God? Those who are being led by the Spirit. "For you have not received a spirit of slavery leading to fear again, but you have received a spirit of adoption as sons by which we cry out, 'Abba! Father!' " (Romans 8:15 NASB). It comes from within: "Father!"

We use a psychological method in some of our soul-winning. We take the Bible and we say, "You are a sinner because the Bible says, 'All have sinned and fall short of the glory of God' (Romans 3:23 NASB). Do you believe that? You have to believe it."

"Yes, yes, yes, I believe it."

"All right. Your works cannot save you because it is written here, 'It's not by works.' Do you believe that? It's the Bible. You have to believe it because it is the Bible, the Word of God." "And you can have eternal life if you believe in the Lord Jesus Christ. You can be saved. Do you believe that?"

"Yes."

"Now don't have doubt. If anyone tells you that you are not saved, remember this verse."

You know, you don't need to use that psychological treatment. Just let him receive the Spirit. And the Spirit will make him say, "Father! My Father!"

"What happened?"

"I don't know. But I know that I am a son of God."

"How do you know?"

"I don't know what to say, but I know!"

"The Spirit Himself bears witness with our spirit that we are children of God" (Romans 8:16 NASB).

"How do you know that you are saved?"

"Well, I forgot the verse . . ." No!

"I know because I have something within me that tells me that I am . . . I am . . . I am a son of God. I know because I know it. It is like a well of living water that springs up."

I want you to see 2 Corinthians 3: 3-6 in the Phillips translation:

You are an open letter about Christ which we ourselves have written, not with pen and ink but with the Spirit of the living God. Our message has been engraved not in stone, but in living men and women.

We dare say such things because of the confidence we have in God through Christ. Not that we are in any way confident of our own resources — our ability comes from God. It is he who makes us competent administrators of the new agreement, and we deal not in the letter but in the Spirit. The letter of the Law leads to the death of the soul; the Spirit of God alone can give life to the soul.

Now look at the King James translation. This is something I had never seen before. "Forasmuch as ye are manifestly declared to be the epistle of Christ ..." Who is the epistle of Christ? Who are the epistles? The believers. They are walking Bibles, walking letters. Paul doesn't say, "You have the epistles under your arm in a book," but he says, You are the epistles of Christ "ministered by us, written not with ink, but with the Spirit of the living God" (2 Corinthians 3:3 KJV).

The apostle wrote that he was the penholder, but the Holy Spirit was the ink. Can a pen write without ink? A pen without ink is the same as a guitar without strings, or a book without pages, or a car without a motor. So then the Holy Spirit is the ink, and the people we minister to are the paper. This is rather new. It is the new covenant!

9

Rivers of Living Water

Now on the last day, the great day of the feast, Jesus stood and cried out, saying, "If any man is thirsty, let him come to Me and drink. He who believes in Me, as the Scripture said, 'From his innermost being shall flow rivers of living water.'" But this He spoke of the Spirit, whom those who believed in Him were to receive. . . .

John 7:37-39 NASB

If any one thirst—thirst for what? Thirst to be able to do God's will! If anyone is thirsty, desiring to do God's will, but unable to manage it—here is a good deal for you! "He that believeth in Me, rivers of living water will flow from within. That is the Spirit I am going to send. It's the promise of the Father."

Jesus said this would happen "as the Scripture said," and there is no one verse in the Old Testament where it says just that. Jesus is not quoting a verse. He is quoting the whole Old Testament. His promise is from Genesis to Malachi. The Scriptures are full of this promise. The prophets spoke about this thing: those who believe in God shall have a new heart, a new spirit within.

Jesus didn't say, "He that believeth on Me shall have the right doctrine"—but rivers! What have you? A right declaration of faith? Or do you have the rivers? The promise of the Father is the rivers from within.

Jesus said the same thing in John 4:13,14, "Everyone who drinks of this water shall thirst again; but whoever drinks of the water that I shall give him shall never thirst; but the water that I shall give him shall become in him a well of water springing up to eternal life" (NASB).

It's a fountain! What have you? A book under your arm, or a fountain within? There are lots of people who have the Bible under one arm, and a book of doctrine under the other. But they have not the river, they have not the fountain. And salvation is a fount, a river in Christ.

Jesus said, "And I will pray the Father, and he shall give you another Comforter, that he may abide with you for ever; even the Spirit of truth; whom the world cannot receive, because it seeth him not, neither knoweth him; for he dwelleth with you and shall be in you. I will not leave you comfortless: I will come to you" (John 14:16-18 KJV).

What Jesus is saying here about the promise of the Father is this, "In times of old, you were under the letter. You were guided by the Law and by rules. Now I have come and you are guided by Me. I show you the way. Soon I will go, but I will send you another Comforter, the Spirit of truth, and He will guide you into all truth.

"Before I came, you lived under the Law. Now you are living under Me. After I am risen, I am going to put you back again under the Law."

Did He say that? No! That would be to go backwards. It would be regressive. And God's revelation is always progressive, from glory to glory.

They were no longer under the Law after Jesus came. For Jesus is greater than the Law. Which is greater? The Law or the Author of the Law?

Then He said, "It is expedient for you that I go away ..."(John 16:7 KJV). "It is to your advantage that I go away"(John 16:7 NASB). Why? Because "now I am *with* you, but then I will be *in* you and that is better." So He went to heaven and sent the promise of the Father. Pentecost came and the Holy Spirit was in them. Jesus' promise came true: "My Father will love him, and We will come to him, and make Our abode with him" (John 14:23 NASB).

When He left them, they had no Sunday school materials, no cassettes, no New Testament, no Bible seminary to send the pastors to; they had the promise of the Father. That is how they were learning and growing and being guided. The good news was spreading over the world! They had reality.

"For the Law, since it has only a shadow of the good things to come and not the very form of things, can never by the same sacrifices year by year, which they offer continually, make perfect those who draw near" (Hebrews 10:1 NASB).

The written Law is the shadow of the reality. The reality is the Spirit. It is the dynamic, actual, working Spirit of Christ. The letter cannot make perfect. But the reality, yes! The Spirit can make perfect—that was the promise of the Father. "I will show you how to walk in My ways and you will keep My ordinances."

So the letter is just a shadow. Suppose I invite you, and you come to Argentina to visit. I am going to give you a nice dinner—turkey. So you come to my house and I seat you at the table. Then I put the turkey on the window sill, and the sun throws the shadow of the turkey on the table. And I say, "Help yourself to the shadow!" You are hungry. What kind of food is that? Just more hunger!

When I read the Scriptures, this Holy Book, I become very hungry to have the things this Book speaks about. When I put the turkey on the table—a-a-a-a-ah! That is what satisfies, not the shadow of it!

Wherever I go I have my wife's picture. Every time I pack my suitcase, my wife makes sure that I have the picture. I set it up in my room on the table, and every night I look at the picture and write a letter. One letter a day goes to Martha. But suppose when I come home, I keep on looking at the picture, writing letters, and don't pay any attention to her?

She would say, "Juan, give me back that picture. I'm here!"

I think Jesus is tired of our obsession with His picture when He is alive and with us. He said, "Lo, I am with you always—until the end of the world." And as far as I know, the end of the world hasn't come yet.

We are living in a day when Jesus is the "I am" for us. I am! "For where two or three have gathered together in My name, there *I am* in their midst" (Matthew 18:20 NASB). "*I am* the true vine . . . you are the branches" (John 15:1, 5 NASB). "*I am* the light of the world; he who follows Me shall not walk in the darkness, but shall have the light of life" (John 8: 12 NASB). And there are many more. Be careful. Pictures are good, but not to be worshiped. They are not more important than the Person. The picture is the shadow of the real Person. Thou shalt not make images!

Suppose you want to build a house and you have the

blueprint. Here is the kitchen, and here is one bedroom, and another, and two bathrooms. Very nice. But that blueprint is not the house. You cannot live in the blueprint! You have conferences over the blueprint. Fine. But where is the house? It is good to have a blueprint to build a house, but it is not good just to enjoy the blueprint! We need more than that.

When we are growing and bearing the fruit of the Spirit, the letter of the Law becomes our servant. The same thing happened with Hagar and Sarah, as Paul told us in Galatians. Hagar is a type of the Law, Sarah of the Spirit. Hagar brought forth slaves, Sarah brought forth free sons. You know what happened in that home. Hagar was needed there; she was the servant, the maid of Sarah. She was under Sarah, but when she noticed that her son was growing, she was ambitious for him, and she wanted to become more important than Sarah. If she and her son had behaved properly and stayed under Sarah, they would not have been cast out. But she wanted to be queen of the house, and she wanted her son to be the heir.

So God said to Abraham, "Listen to Sarah and oust Hagar" (Galatians 4:30). When the letter is in its place, it is under the Spirit. But when it wants to rule and put us under bondage, making us Ishmaels and not Isaacs, be careful! God will say to oust her, "For the son of the bondwoman shall not be an heir with the son of the free woman" (Galatians 4:30 NASB).

Sarah is a type of the Jerusalem that comes down from above, of the new heart, the life in the Spirit. The whole letter to the Galatians is very clear on this. We get confused when we think that Hagar represents the Old Testament and Sarah the New Testament. Hagar represents the letter and Sarah the Spirit that comes from above, the Jerusalem which is free and brings forth free sons.

Isaacs are those people born by the Spirit without any

human help. Why did God wait so long to give that child Isaac to them? Why couldn't Abraham have had the promise as soon as he believed? Because God wanted to be sure that everyone was convinced that neither Abraham nor Sarah could have children. They waited and waited— until when? Until Abraham's body was "dead." If Sarah had had a child when she was younger, people would have said, "She is not barren." But she was barren and had no child all her life. It was not until she was old and everybody knew it was impossible that the child Isaac came! There was to be no doubt at all but that the child was from above.

But Ishmael? Who knows? He was a mixture. Of course, I am speaking spiritually. If you are an Ishmaelite according to the flesh, we love you very much through Jesus Christ, and we are of the same family of God now. Jesus died on the cross to tear down the middle wall of all partitions. But Ishmael is a type of the letter which brings forth bondslaves, people under the Law. Sarah brings forth those who are born of the Spirit and live by the promise of the Father.

Jesus, when He was resurrected, and about to return to heaven, gathered His disciples. "He commanded them not to leave Jerusalem, but to wait for what the Father had promised, 'Which,' He said, 'you heard of from Me'" (Acts 1:4 NASB). What was this promise that they received on the day of Pentecost?

The promise of the Father is the whole life in the Spirit. It is not just the speaking in tongues. Speaking in other languages was just the bell ringing, br-r-r-r-r, that announced that the promise had come! So I do not believe any more in "the baptism in the Holy Spirit according to Acts 2:4," but in the baptism of the Spirit according to Genesis through Revelation. The whole promise!

What is the reality of this new covenant? It is the reality

of the Spirit of God actually performing within a person what the shadow indicated He would do. It is the fruit of the Spirit of God worked out and visible in life. It is love, joy, peace, longsuffering, gentleness, goodness, faith, meekness, and temperance. Against such things there is no law!

True, there is a kind of love born by the Law, but that love is out of the flesh, of dead works. Read Hebrews 9:14. You can give your body to be burned and all your possessions to the poor, but if it doesn't come by the fruit of the Spirit, God doesn't accept it. The Law brings forth slaves who want to rule. But the sons of Hagar will not inherit the promise. The sort of love brought forth by Hagar is of the flesh and out of commandments.

What are the things born of the flesh? They are all the things we do by law. The things born of the Spirit are the result of the life of God in us. The letter operates through our effort and its threat. The Spirit of Christ operates through our faith and His grace.

Keep out of debt altogether, except that perpetual debt of love which we owe one another. The man who loves his neighbor has obeyed the whole Law in regard to his neighbor. For the commandments, "Thou shalt not commit adultery," "Thou shalt not kill," "Thou shalt not steal," "Thou shalt not covet" and all other commandments are summed up in this one saying: "Thou shalt love thy neighbor as thyself." Love hurts nobody: therefore love is the answer to the Law's commands.

Romans 13:8-10 J. B. Phillips

What is the fulfillment of the Law? *Love.* And love is much, much more than the fulfillment of the Law. It goes far beyond the Law. The Law said, "Thou shalt not covet," but the Law never demanded, "Thou shalt have peace, thou shalt have meekness." Never. The fruit of the Spirit is much, much more.

That is why Paul said to the Galatians, "Are you so foolish? Having begun by the Spirit, are you now being perfected by the flesh?" (Galatians 3:3 NASB). He was worried that they were turning back to the Law. They had started in the Spirit. "Did you receive the Spirit by the works of the Law, or by hearing with faith?" (Galatians 3:2 NASB).

If there is one thing important in Scripture, it is the new covenant and the promise of the Father which we are to receive. And the fruit of the Spirit comes from this new life, not from a new set of laws. Every time we drink the wine of the Lord's Supper we say, "This is the cup of the new covenant." This is what it means: Jesus died and shed His blood to bring us into the new covenant and to deliver us forever from the dead works of the Law. If we do not know what the new covenant is, then what does that ceremony mean for us?

The fruit of the Spirit not only fulfills more than the written requirements, but it also pleases God. Why? Because it is no longer a burden to walk in His way; the enabling comes from inside. It is like rivers of living water.

"Why do you love me? You have every reason not to!"

"Because I can't help but love you."

"Why? It's unreasonable."

"Because the Spirit within enables me. I am sorry, brother, but I love you. I don't like to love you, but I just do love you."

The Spirit Himself produces the fruit, with no help from us. If you have the love, joy, peace, longsuffering, gentleness, faith, meekness and temperance, you won't be worried about tongues. You do anything when you are full of love. If you go where they are dancing in the Spirit, you dance. If you go into a quiet, ritualistic service, you do not criticize, you feel the presence of Jesus there. If you go anywhere full of the Spirit, you will come out loving.

Do you think that God is a liar when He said, "A new heart will I give you and My Spirit within?" No! That's what they received on Pentecost. Suddenly the promise of the Father came, and they received the Holy Spirit, the promise they were waiting for, the new covenant, a new interior life that started to guide them.

What was the result? They stayed together; they prayed; they loved everyone; they were fearless; they had fellowship with one another. Miracles were done. They lived together. They had their things in common. They sold their property and goods and brought the proceeds to the feet of the apostles. They shared with all who were in need. They persevered in accord. They ate together. Their love was contagious and worth dying for. What came naturally to them was much, much more than the requirements of the Law.

The Law never asked them to sell their goods. The Law never said they had to live together, to perform miracles, to go into all the world and be expendable for others. Never. This life in the Spirit is much more than the Law, because Pentecost is the reality foreshadowed. It is the new heart, with God's desires built in, with the Trinity at home in the heart. It is rivers of living water flowing out to every community and nation.

When I think of the greatness of this great plan I fall on my knees before the Father . . . and I pray that out of the glorious richness of his resources he will enable you to know the strength of the Spirit's inner reinforcement—that Christ may actually live in your hearts by your faith. And I pray that you, firmly fixed in love yourselves, may be able to grasp (with all

Christians) how wide and deep and long and high is
the love of Christ—and to know for yourselves that
love so far beyond our comprehension. May you be
filled through all your being with God Himself!

Ephesians 3:14-19 J. B. Phillips

Then your light will rise in darkness,
And your gloom will become like midday.
And the Lord will continually guide you,
And satisfy your desire in scorched places,
and give strength to your bones;
And you will be like a watered garden,
And like a spring of water whose waters do not fail.
And those from among you will rebuild the ancient
     ruins;
You will raise up the age-old foundations;
And you will be called the repairer of the breach,
The restorer of the streets in which to dwell.

Isaiah, 58:10-12 NASB

10

Schoolmasters

We have talked much about the abuses of the Scriptures. I want to be very clear on one point at this time. I do not in any way mean to downgrade the Bible. Praise the Lord for the Scriptures! They are indispensable to us from beginning to end. They are the picture, the shadow which leads us to the reality of God. Paul calls the Word of God a schoolmaster to bring us into the knowledge of the One who lives within us.

What a wonderful schoolmaster! A child may say in third grade, "I have the best teacher in the world; I don't want to go on into fourth grade!" But this would grieve the third-grade teacher. He wouldn't want it.

"For all who are being led by the Spirit of God, these are

sons of God" (Romans 8:14 NASB). It is then that the Scriptures come to us confirming the way the Spirit has led. What greater joy does a schoolmaster have than to see his pupil grown and living fully the life school was preparing him for. Then he can become the friend, confidant and counselor to his onetime pupil and they can smile together about the things that happened in school. To be in school is not bad, but to stay forever in third grade would be sad.

Paul says, "The law was our schoolmaster to bring us unto Christ . . . but after that faith is come, we are no longer under a schoolmaster" (Galatians 3:24, 25 KJV).

The original meaning of the word for *schoolmaster* can include the practice of pounding a stick into the ground beside a small tree. The tree is tied to the stick so that the wind won't push it over. But when the tree is grown, the stick is not necessary to hold it. At first, the stick holds the tree. Afterward, the tree holds the stick!

Under the Law, the people of Israel had to do what the Law said. In the old covenant the Scriptures made the people. As I have said before, the people of the new covenant, full of the Spirit, made the Scriptures. What I mean is this: we now joyfully seek the spirit behind the letter more than the letter for its own sake.

David was in touch with God. He played the harp, he spoke with God in songs and dialogs. He knew the Law, and he also knew the Maker of the Law. He said, "O how I love Thy law! It is my meditation all the day" (Psalm 119:97 NASB). But he also had dealings with God: "Why hast Thou forgotten me?" (Psalm 42:9 NASB). "Answer me quickly, O Lord, my spirit fails; do not hide Thy face from me" (Psalm 143:7 NASB).

For David, it was a continual life in the Spirit with God. Once David got to a place and he was very hungry. He went to the house of the priests because he liked to be with holy men. He felt comfortable in the presence of such men.

When he got there, he said, "I'm hungry. Have you any bread?"

The priest said, "Oh, the only bread we have is the holy bread, and it is just for priests."

In his heart David said, *What do you think, God? Eat,* said God.

"Bring the bread!" David took it, blessed it, gave thanks to God for the bread and ate it.

Jesus said to the Pharisees, "Don't you remember what David did when he went to the priests' house, and there was nothing other than holy bread? Don't you know what he did?" (Matthew 12:3, 4).

Silence. The spirit of the law about the loaves was that this bread was a type of the Lord Jesus, the true bread from heaven. David had the permission of the Writer of the Law.

You remember that Jesus once healed a man who had been sick a long time and told him, "Take your bed and go home."

He took the bed on the Sabbath. So some letter-bound people said, "Oh oh! This is the Sabbath."

"I know," he said, "the best Sabbath of my life!" They knew the law of the Sabbath but not the spiritual Sabbath rest. God had worked on that Sabbath for that man. That was a real day of rest for him. After thirty-eight years of working days, he got to his Sabbath. But the other people were letter-centered.

"Who authorized you to pick up your bed?"

"Oh, I was so excited that I didn't find out who it was." Tremendous! This is the spirit of the Word! Let me explain it another way.

In my country two years ago, a very poor woman went into a supermarket. She bought bread and milk and stole a piece of meat, putting it in her purse. When she was going out at the counter, she paid for the bread and milk.

Then she was told, "Open your purse!"

She didn't want to, but the police came and she had to open the purse. The meat was there. So she was taken to the police station and then to the court to stand before the judge. In my country, only the judge can use the penal code to judge people. (They are not as foolish as religious people where everybody has the penal code and judges others with the authority of the letter!) Not even the police can judge, but only the judges, because they are the makers of the law and not only know the law, but the spirit behind the law.

The judge talked gently with the poor woman and found out that she had been abandoned by her husband and had five children. They had no house and had had no good food for months. So what did he do? Instead of sending her to jail, he gave her a modest house and ordered a pension for her. To this judge, the spirit of the law was more important than the law. For the supermarket owner and the police, the law was more important.

In the matter of the woman taken in adultery in the book of John, Jesus acted to thwart the legalistic people who were about to strike her. He was the Maker of the Law, and He knew the hearts of men and women. He knew the circumstances and the repentance in the woman.

He said to her, "Neither do I condemn you; go your way; from now on sin no more" (John 8:11 NASB). He saved the woman and did it against the Law, you might say. But the spirit of the Law was there!

We have a Bible in the hands of "children" and each one considers himself a judge. Give knives and guns to children and see what happens. In our house we don't leave matches lying on the table. It is dangerous. But in my mother-in-law's house there are only older people and the matches are anywhere. There is no danger. Why? Because no children are there. A thing is dangerous or not according to the level of growth.

I understand the dangers of what I am saying, but I believe that nothing can be more dangerous than the current situation of the Church.

In the early Church for years and years—we can say until the 16th century—the Bible was not in the hands of all the believers. There was no printing equipment before the 15th century, so it would have been impossible. Not even every church had a Bible, and so the Bible was unknown to many followers of Christ for sixteen centuries. That was dangerous, because all the authority stayed in the hands of the leaders of the Church. Idolatry, false doctrines, superstition came into the Church and nobody could say, "Be careful," because nobody had the Bible.

Was it dangerous for Christians to be for sixteen centuries without the Bible? Very dangerous. And you know what happened? It brought the Reformation with Martin Luther and a break that could have been avoided.

We say, "Praise the Lord! The Bible is now translated into the language of the people and everybody has a Bible in his hand." Is that not also dangerous? From the first, people started quarreling. Divisions, denominations, and groups emerged here and there. The free interpretation of the Bible has brought a Babel of confusion. Is not that a danger? We have Jehovah's Witnesses, Mormons, Universalists, Evangelicals, Liberals, and Fundamentalists. Before the Bible was given, we had one fold. Now we have many folds. From the Bible and a concordance you can build up the doctrine for each one.

In a small group someone disagrees about something and says, "I will start a new church."

"What authority do you have?"

"The authority of the Bible!"

In Chile I went to a city of 13,000 people. There were fifteen churches there. I was sent by Evangelism in Depth to organize a campaign and called all the ministers together. There was such quarreling among them that all that joined the campaign were a Pentecostal church and one division of the Baptists.

Each minister said, "If they go into it, we don't go." But everybody was under the authority of the Bible! Is that not dangerous?

We don't see the danger we are in. Somebody tells me, "Ortiz, what you are saying is dangerous!" Dear friends, what we have is dangerous, as dangerous as if we were in a big ship that is sinking. The water is up to my knees and I think, *Goodbye, life!*

Suddenly, a helicopter comes over and they call down to me, "Johnny, here's a rope ladder! Grab it and come up!"

But people around me say, "Don't go to the helicopter! Helicopters are very dangerous!"

Do you understand? What is more dangerous than the situation we are in? We have tried unity in the Scriptures. Let us now try unity in the Spirit and see how God works.

The Bible is not guilty. The Bible is the inspired record of the revelation of Jesus Christ. But we need to know the Author of it, have fellowship with Him and live close to Him in order to understand what He means.

When you receive a telegram that is not clear, there can be many different interpretations. But if you know the sender well enough and the whole situation, you can know of a certainty what he means. There can be many different interpretations of the written Word, but the living Word does not have two meanings. I know when God says "No!" I cannot explain it, but I know it. When God says, "Yes," I know it too; it is when I have the peace of God.

What is the spirit of the letter? Paul says in 1 Corinthians 2:15, 16 that the spiritual man judges everything, but he himself is judged of no man. Who can judge the one who has the mind of Christ? We need to know more than the letter of the Bible to be men and women of God.

11

Sound Doctrine

I know an ignorant woman in my country who is more truly a theologian than many of those who are called theologians. What is theology? *Theos* means God, and so it is the study of God Himself.

Some confusion exists here. What we study in seminaries is not truly theology but "Bible-ology." I am not saying Bible-ology is wrong. Praise the Lord for the Bible and the study of the Bible, but let us call things by the right name.

However, the "ignorant" woman I referred to is one who has dealings with God. She knows Him and speaks with Him every day. She is a friend of His. That is why I call her a theologian. One of the Church fathers said, "A theologian is one who prays."

Only the Holy Spirit can teach you theology. Jesus said,

"He (the Holy Spirit) shall receive of Mine and show it unto you" (John 16:15). Only those who have the promise of the Father dwelling in their hearts can be theologians in the truest sense. And there is another prerequisite for the study of God.

I beseech you, brethren, by the mercies of God, that you present your bodies a living sacrifice to God. Do not conform to this world. But be ye transformed by the renewing of your mind that you may experience the perfect will of God (Romans 12:1,2).

What is the requirement for experiencing God's will? To present our bodies as a living sacrifice. That is death. God can do whatever He wants with us, dead or alive. A sacrifice is a lamb laid on the altar and killed. What is a "living" sacrifice? God says, "Put the lamb on the altar, but don't kill it." He will do whatever He likes with it.

You are a living sacrifice. God can send you wherever He wants. You are not going to say no. He can reveal Himself to you, and through you. You are His.

Then, you are not conformed to the world. We are not conformists. It is amazing how the ways of the world can invade God's called-out people. Maybe you think this is just in externals. No! The spirit of the world is the individualistic spirit, the capitalistic spirit, the humanistic spirit. Those are ways of the world, too.

Third, you are transformed by the renewing of your mind. When you are being transformed, you are not the same today as yesterday. Tomorrow the metamorphosis will continue. That is because of the renewing of your mind. That renewing is costly in the changes it makes. And then God is going to reveal His perfect will. Can God show His will to a person who will not change, one who is like a train that will never go off the tracks? Our dogmas are settled; the doctrines cannot be changed. We are like a merry-go-round, like children sitting in a little car. We can move the wheel, but it is fastened to the merry-go-round and always goes around the same way.

Lord, show us Your will! But we are not going to change. We want to go on singing the same songs, saying the same prayers, hearing the same messages over and over. Then how can God show us His will?

Jesus did not come to teach a new philosophy, but to bring a new life; not a new thought but a new spirit, a new attitude. He came to give us God's point of view in every detail of life.

What did Jesus teach? He went to a party and saw this Pharisee come in looking for the best seat.

So Jesus said, "You see that? Don't do like that. When you come to a party, take the lowest chair."

Did He spend time teaching about the millennium or the Trinity? No. This was His doctrine: Don't take the best chairs, take the lowest chairs. And listen, when you make a banquet, don't call those who can pay you back with another feast. Call the poor, the blind, the beggars, those who cannot return anything to you, and your Father will return it to you from heaven (Luke 14:7-14).

Paul, when he wrote letters, did not usually lay out a system of doctrine, but he wrote according to the needs of the people. He gave them the answer God gave him for their present situation. He was sharing what he knew of God's perfect will.

It is after we grow up, that we can come to our parents and say, "O Mom, O Dad, now I understand why you spanked me so many times. Thank you! Now I understand why you did it!" This is because now we are fathers ourselves.

It is after some spiritual growth that we can say to God, "Now, dear Father, I understand Your burden. O forgive me! Dear God, now I see it from Your point of view. Now I see Your kingdom as You see it!"

He will keep renewing our minds. He will give us His heart, and we will grow into the father's position spiritually. We will find ourselves talking with Him as father to Father. We will have His feelings.

This is when the Scriptures really come alive and confirm the word of the Spirit which we have heard in our hearts. Alleluia! The Bible is the builder's plumbline that assures the straightness of the building and keeps it from leaning to the right or left.

It is great when we begin to have the mind and heart of the Father. The Father doesn't take sides and neither will we. In Argentina a great deal of the denominational work has come out of divisions. Someone has estimated by computer that in our day the new groups get divided once every six years! Suddenly, in a group of elders, someone will start to accuse the pastor. Others excuse and uphold him. They hold meetings and another division comes. What God wants is so different!

But now in Christ Jesus you who formerly were far off have been brought near by the blood of Christ. For He Himself is our peace, who made both groups into one, and broke down the barrier of the dividing wall, by abolishing in His flesh the enmity, which is the Law of commandments contained in ordinances, that in Himself He might make the two into one new man, thus establishing peace, and might reconcile them both in one body to God through the cross, by it having put to death the enmity.

Ephesians 2:13-16 NASB

You remember when Paul and Barnabas quarreled about John Mark? Paul with Silas went one way and Barnabas with Mark went another way. But the fellowship of believers didn't take sides, because it acted as a mother.

We need the parental touch. A kingdom-minded follower has the Father's point of view. One son leaves, like the prodigal, and his father waits for him. When he comes back, the father is glad. There is a feast. The other son gets angry.

If one of us had been that father, we might have said, "So? You are angry because of your brother's return? Then you get out of here!" But that would be winning the one and losing the other!

This father said to the angry one, "Come in," and to the prodigal, "Don't pay attention to your brother, he's going to be convinced." That's the Father!

Another thing we have when we have a kingdom mind is freedom. Paul talks about financial support for himself in 1 Corinthians nine and ten. He knew he was worthy of financial support, but he didn't take it. Even if offered it, he would have declined. Why? Because he wanted to be free, not independent, but free. If he took support from the Jewish group, they would put strings on him.

They would call him into the office very often for board meetings and say, "We hear that you are preaching among the Gentiles. We want you to preach to the Jews."

He didn't take support from the Gentiles, because he wanted also to be free to go to Jerusalem and to the Jewish temple. So he says,

> What then is my reward? That, when I preach the gospel, I may offer the gospel without charge, so as not to make full use of my right in the gospel. For though I am free from all men, I have made myself a slave to all, that I might win the more.
>
> I Corinthians 9:18,19 NASB

This is a real motivation to be free. Paul wanted to be free in order to be servant to all. Some people like to be free to do their own will. That's psychological, independent freedom. He is speaking here of spiritual freedom. He was free to be a servant both to the Jews and the Gentiles. He could go to the Jewish ceremonies, and he could eat with the Gentiles.

> And to the Jews I became as a Jew, that I might win Jews; to those who are under the Law, as under the Law, though not being myself under the Law, that I might win those who are under the Law; to those who are without law, as without law, though not being without the law of God *but under the law of Christ,* that I might win those who are without law. To the weak I became weak, that I might win the weak; I have become all things to all men, that I may by all means save some.
>
> I Corinthians 9:20-22 NASB

To the weak who don't drink wine or eat meat, I become weak, that is, I don't drink wine or eat meat, that I may win them, says Paul. I also become all things to all men that I may by all means save some. To Lutherans I become as a Lutheran; to Episcopalians, as an Episcopalian.

If I should move from my country and live in England, I would apply to be an Anglican minister. That's the best in England. The cream of society is in that church. The Queen goes to it, the prime minister and the parliament members go there, so I should go there. If I should move to Norway, I would become a Lutheran minister.

So Paul, when he went to Jerusalem was free to shave his head, or free to leave his hair as it was. No problem. We have problems only when we are not truly free. Christ's freedom is within us, independent of external circumstances.

Then, when we are really free in Christ, all things belong to us. When Paul was writing to the Corinthians about the jealousy and strife among them, he said:

> What then is Apollos? And what is Paul? Servants through whom you believed, even as the Lord gave opportunity to each one. I planted, Apollos watered, but God was causing the growth. So then neither the one who plants nor the one who waters is anything, but God who causes the growth. . . . So then let no one boast in men. For all things belong to you, whether Paul or Apollos or Cephas or the world or life or death or things present or things to come; all things belong to you, and you belong to Christ; and Christ belongs to God.
>
> I Corinthians 3:5-7, 21-23 NASB

I feel myself to be such a rich man now. Sometimes we buy cookies from the bakery and there are a dozen, each different, and having four children we say, "There are three each." So then there is a fight about who is going to choose first. After that, they fight because someone else got the one with jam on it. I often wonder how one of them would feel if he were given all twelve cookies for himself alone!

I don't have to choose, because all denominations are mine. I am a very wealthy person. All the Lutherans are mine. All the Pentecostals are mine. All the nice Episcopalian church buildings are mine and their quiet services. All the shouting services are mine too. I am sorry for you if you have to choose between them. I'm a very lucky person. All are mine.

If you have a kingdom mind, there is no envy. You hear the Pentecostal brethren are enlarging their work? Praise the Lord! When the Presbyterians ordain more pastors—praise the Lord! When the Lutherans have a nice building—praise the Lord! I used to be very much against Catholics and my church had no nice retreat place in the country. But now, since we love Catholics, we use their nice, big conference grounds—very inexpensive.

The unity of the Body of Christ is very close to the Father's heart. But while much of the Church views ecumenicism in terms of organizational structure, God has in view a spiritual unity. In the shadow of those great ecumenical councils snarled in doctrinal wrangling, blocked by irreconcilable viewpoints, God is working out this spiritual unity. The Spirit's ecumenical movement is bringing brothers and sisters of all faiths together all over the world to celebrate the Lordship of Christ and to express the joy of their common faith.

12

Fresh Daily

I am not afraid any more if a Jehovah's Witness or Mormon team visits my church members because now my people have life. Between life and death there is a vast difference. These cults have many false ideas, according to us, and we were always afraid that if our people got a wrong concept, they would go astray. So we were very careful and overprotected them—like keeping them in a greenhouse. We wanted them to avoid anybody else who might preach to them something different, because salvation seemed to depend on having the right concepts.

But, praise the Lord, we see things in a different light now. We are no more children tossed to and fro by any wind of doctrine. We are growing, and our people are skillful too in the word of righteousness and in hearing the voice of Him who is life, life flowing from our innermost being. Our conscience leads us and life is completely different. Strange concepts we don't fear at all. Many concepts come, but the life within us has no problems with wrong doctrines.

I've seen in Japan and in Muslim countries that Christians feel they are in a battle—their concepts against Buddhist or Muslim concepts. Do we need to put Buddhist concepts and our concepts in the balance to show that ours are better? The crux of the matter is not concepts against concepts. It is the life, the Spirit within us, versus concepts. It's not the Bible against the Koran. It is Jesus Christ, the living One, against false concepts. False religious concepts are small stones in the path of the mighty river of life in Christ Jesus.

Jesus did not say, "I go to heaven, but I leave you a Book. Here is a concordance and commentaries, so entertain yourselves. Bye-bye!" NO! He said, "Lo, I am with you always" (Matthew 28:20 NASB).

He is the only Founder of religion that is still alive with His people. If Jesus is not alive, we are at a continual funeral. What do people do at funerals? They speak about the person who has passed away—what he did, what he said when he was alive, everything from his death on back to his birth. Sometimes our churches look like funerals and sound like them.

I am amazed when I read the epistles. The epistles are messages Jesus gave the apostles for that moment. They are not commentaries on the Gospels. Paul never said to Timothy, "Please read John 10. Now I am going to comment on 'I am the door.' It means this and that. 'To come in and go out' means this and that. Now read the passage on Zacchaeus. The tree means this." Never! Paul never worked that way. He had the living Jesus within.

Paul would ask Jesus, "What do you want to tell the Church today?"

And Jesus would say to Paul, "This is what I want you to tell them today."

Jesus was alive within him. "Lo, I am with you always!" What have you? A religion or the living presence of Jesus?

The living Jesus is a problem to our religious institutions. Yes. Because if you are having a funeral, a nice funeral, and the dead person starts to move, there goes the funeral! And, dear brothers and sisters, Jesus is moving!

In a cemetery you can maintain a grave for years and years in the same way. It never changes. The structure of cemeteries is always the same. But if the dead should come alive, I think the cemetery would change a little bit.

I have recently seen more than ever before what a problem it is causing to the Church to be concept-centered rather than Spirit-centered. The trip to Japan helped me to understand this. I had the opportunity to visit some temples, Buddhist and Hindu, and also to read about Buddha in the book that is placed, along with the Gideon Bible, in every hotel room. I found that we also have a religion with a Founder who died and left in a Book His thoughts. Those thoughts we try to think, too, and it is possible for us to have just a conceptual religion and no dynamic life.

I think that the difference between the church club and the kingdom of God is that the church club is concept-centered. To get into one, we need to accept its philosophical definition of its beliefs, or what is called theological concepts, and also whatever other requirements they have, such as not smoking. But these requirements differ from one denomination to another.

Usually, by simply accepting a denomination's concepts, you can become a member. But in the kingdom of God it is a question of life. You can be a member of a church club by filling out an application or going to the front in a meeting, but entrance into the kingdom is only by birth. And at birth, a life starts. So the kingdom is a matter of life; for many churches, it is a matter of concepts. And that makes a great difference. To some, this thought is frightening because they are so bound to concepts that when something else is being preached, they see their whole religious system coming down.

The structured church appears to be in competition with the kingdom of God. It has taken over the kingdom's language and names. Church members call one another "brother," but often they are not brothers. They say, "Jesus lives within us," but many times He doesn't, or they don't really recognize it. People can sing in a service "Since Jesus came into my heart." Then the same people in the same service sing next "Come into my heart, Lord Jesus!" They don't really understand what life is all about. Which do they mean?

Entering the kingdom is a matter of life, not of an intellectual concept. We are not going to get into the kingdom by having the proper concept of the Trinity or any other issue. We go in by birth, and then we are alive and we grow. What is life? Life is love, joy, peace, longsuffering, gentleness, goodness, faith, meekness, temperance. That's life! He who loves is born of God. In the kingdom, it is a question of life and death, not of right concepts or wrong concepts.

Notice that when Evangelicals are fighting among themselves, or Jehovah's Witnesses are fighting against Evangelicals, they are pitting concepts against concepts. We don't need to fight at all if we are living the life.

It is also sad to notice that things that come from life can be made into dogmas and become things to fight over. In our country, discipleship and submission were concepts that evolved out of life. Then I began to put them on the blackboard and it looked very mechanical. You see, people have conceptualized today what was life yesterday! Life, real life in the Spirit, can be made into a doctrine or concept, and then you live by the concept. This is what Paul calls beginning in the Spirit and then following in the flesh (Galatians 3:3).

The important thing is: What does the Spirit want to stress in a certain group? At one time I came into a group of lonely individuals each doing his own thing—independents. And I preached about submission. Later I came to them and had to say, "Brothers, be careful with this doctrine of submission!"

Was I contradicting myself? No, I was just trying to be led by the Spirit to say what needed to be said. I believe in submission with all my heart, but when people make submission a legalistic doctrine and start to divide the Body of Christ with it, I say, "Wait a moment! Let's see the other side." So the Spirit is the One who always has the living word for each situation.

When we make the life of the Spirit a law, then we become legalists. Legalism is nothing other than conceptualizing what yesterday the Spirit told us. So much of the Church today is legalistic because the life in the Spirit, demonstrated in the Acts of the Apostles and in the epistles, has been conceptualized and now we are living under those concepts. On the other hand, the people to whom Paul was writing were living by the life of Jesus and receiving the epistles as a revelation from God.

The trouble comes when we live under the concept of submission, for example, and not by the submission given us by the life of the Spirit within us. We preach about discipleship and teach it. Then that becomes a concept and we live by the concept of discipleship, and not by the life of the Spirit.

What is born of the Spirit is spirit and what is born of the flesh is flesh. Even though something was very, very much of God yesterday, today it can be flesh, law, concept. That is the problem we see in the development of church history. Awakenings are conceptualized, and in the next generation they are new denominations, a religion lived by concepts!

Oh, if we could learn the lesson of living by the Spirit! If we could learn the lesson of not making concepts of what the Spirit tells us. If we could only understand that what the Spirit tells us today is for today, and the Spirit will tell us tomorrow what to do tomorrow. We don't need to conceptualize. I am remembering the analogy of the manna in the wilderness. They had to gather only for that day. If they took more, it would be spoiled the next day. That is the life of the Spirit—just like that! The Spirit directs us for today, not for tomorrow. "Therefore do not be anxious for tomorrow; for tomorrow will care for itself" (Matthew 6:34 NASB).

But, of course, if we don't believe that the Spirit will give us enough tomorrow, we will do as some of the Israelites did. We will conceptualize the life in the Spirit. We will put in a box what the life of the Spirit tells us today and keep it in the refrigerator for tomorrow. Then tomorrow we put away some more leftovers, and God hates that. Sometimes yesterday's leftover concepts can be completely opposite to what He has for us today. One of the worst things we can do is not to trust Him to give something fresh every day.

This life in the Spirit of God, fresh daily, is more important than what I was teaching about discipleship and submission. Of course, I understand why God taught us those things. We cannot go on to solid food if we have not first done away with the milk. We have to drink the milk first, and discipleship is only for the purpose of providing milk.

Children are like slaves when they are babes, and the father and mother are the master and mistress. Paul says that a child is no different from a servant when he is a babe (Galatians 4:1). Children are ruled by rules: Don't touch this! Be careful of this! Don't do that! Get up now! Brush your teeth! But a grown-up person does not live by rules. He is led by his inner intelligence, his wider knowledge and his ability to make the proper decision in every situation.

So when we were children and living in the flesh, we needed some rules and discipline. And I think discipleship provides that. A person is taught by submission and discipleship the milk of the Word, that is, the rules about the fixed patterns of conduct on fornication, drunkenness, lying, etc. When he has drunk the milk well, he won't have the wrong guidance as an adult.

Some people fear that when we speak about life in the Spirit, we are on dangerous ground. They think people will start to have funny revelations, do weird things, start to commit things they shouldn't, or go into heresies.

The danger depends on one's maturity. Gas stoves are dangerous. And so when the children were young, we used to turn off the main gas supply valve for the house after we finished cooking. We knew that small children could turn on one of the valves and kill us all. That is because they were children. Adults don't turn the main gas valve off every day if no children are around. Even so, though we may need teaching, rules and precautions when we are babes, we need to go on unto perfection and live this life in the Spirit.

Discipleship is an illustration of life becoming a concept and getting spoiled. In our country we had never heard the word *discipleship*. We had never read a book on it. But in our church, as we were trying to serve God, the Spirit brought to us this idea of having people committed to us, helping and teaching them, living with them, showing them how to live—and there was life.

Then I went throughout the world. I was invited because people saw what was happening in our church. In every place I said, "Brothers, this came to us as life."

But I realized that many people saw it as just a new technique. They took it as a concept, not as life. They asked one another, "Do you believe in discipleship?" And whether the answer was yes or no, it had become a concept, just another doctrine.

If it doesn't come by life, discipleship will spoil your church. We start in the Spirit, and we end up with rules and doctrines. We conceptualize the Spirit. This is very important: the thing the Spirit told us yesterday can be done today in the flesh, by laws. We have become legalistic again.

Perhaps the Spirit tells me today, "Johnny, don't ride on horseback today."

So I say, "Lord, today I won't take the horses." But then tomorrow I tell others what the Lord said to me. I start a group of the "No-Riding-on-Horseback" people. What is the problem? It is that I tell everybody that I forbid the horse. But the Spirit wants to have the preeminence. He wants to tell me every day what to do.

So next day He says, "No cars today, take the horses!" Now what do I do?

It is life in the Spirit that counts. We Pentecostals tend to make a rigid doctrine of the baptism in the Spirit according to Acts 2:4. We forget Acts 2:45—the selling of our possessions. But listen! The same chapter, the same writer, the same Spirit who said, "They were filled with the Holy Spirit, and spake with tongues," also said, "They were filled with the Holy Spirit and sold their possessions." Is it not so?

God sometimes needs to shake and stir us because we

106

are so bound by our traditions and concepts. Peter was told by Jesus Himself, "Arise, Peter, kill and eat!"

His reaction was so conditioned that he answered, "By no means, Lord! I have never eaten anything unholy or unclean" (Acts 10:13,14 NASB).

"So kill and eat!"

"Lord, no!"

So you have life versus concepts. And for people of a conceptual religion, Jesus Christ can become a problem. Jesus Christ was a problem to the religious community that preached His coming, when He came! Because the concept of how the Messiah would come was so strong that when He came as He did, to have accepted Him would have spoiled the concept. So they had to kill the Messiah to maintain the concept intact. Don't forget that He came unto His own, and it was His own who received Him not.

Today we are supposed to be His own, and it is possible that when the living Jesus comes to some of us, we may say, "We are sorry, Jesus, but we have good doctrines and we are all right without You." Of course, we don't say it with our mouths, but really Jesus has little place in many structured churches today. We have everything well settled, and the living Jesus would be a tremendous problem to a church that lives by concepts.

The kingdom of God is life. For this reason, we see in people their life, not their concepts. You know a person can be wrong and have a good spirit. And a person can be right and have a wrong spirit. When you hear a discussion of doctrines, don't see who is "right," but see who has the good spirit. The important thing anyway is our spirit and our knowledge of the heart of God.

Jesus always looked at the spirit behind the external.

But what do you think? A man had two sons, and he came to the first and said, "Son, go work today in the vineyard." And he answered and said, "I will, sir"; and he did not go. And he came to the second and said the same thing. But he answered and said, "I will not"; yet he afterward regretted it and went. Which of the two did the will of his father?

They (the chief priests) said, "The latter."
                                    Matthew 21:28-31 NASB

Once Jesus said to His disciples, "Ye know not what manner of spirit ye are of" (Luke 9:55 KJV). And those were His own disciples! They were defending Him and using Bible verses.

"Do you want us to do as Elijah did?" Elijah called down fire from heaven, and also killed all 400 prophets of Baal. That was the spirit of Elijah.

"But I want you to have My Spirit," Jesus was telling them.

So we have to know more than what men call theology. God wants us to know Jesus Christ, His presence, His life, His mind, His Spirit.

I went to southern Africa not long ago, invited by non-charismatic groups. So the Pentecostals and charismatics came also to see what I would teach these folk.

In one meeting an Anglican asked the question, "Brother, do you believe in rebaptism?"

I said, "Rebaptism? What is that? I have never heard of it."

He said, "When one of the members of our church joins a certain charismatic group in my city for prayer, they teach him to be rebaptized by immersion in water. Do you believe in that?"

Well, I am a Pentecostal. I believe in baptism by immersion and I realized I had myself rebaptized many Lutherans, Anglicans, Methodists and Catholics. So in my heart I cried, *Lord, what should I do here?*

Then Jesus taught me a tremendous lesson, together with all of them. He said, *Read Romans 2!*

> For indeed circumcision is of value, if you practice the Law; but if you are a transgressor of the Law, your circumcision has become uncircumcision. If therefore the uncircumcised man keeps the requirements of the Law, will not his uncircumcision be regarded as circumcision? And will not he who is physically uncircumcised, if he keeps the Law, will he not judge you who though having the letter of the Law and circumcision are a transgressor of the Law?
>
> Romans 2:25-27 NASB

So I said, "Dear brothers, if an un-baptized person lives a baptized life, his nonbaptism is made baptism. And if a baptized person lives a nonbaptized life, his baptism is not baptism." I also said, *Lord, thank You!*

You see how Paul was looking to the spirit and the life and not to concepts. And you know that to the Jews circumcision was a matter of death or life. But Paul says that circumcision is not really what counts. In fact, your circumcision may be counted by God as uncircumcision!

I know many well-baptized Baptists who are not baptized for God, and many nonbaptized who are well baptized according to God's point of view. So it is more than the letter or the religious rite that counts.

What about good works? When God causes us to walk in His ways, then we do unconsciously the good works He has provided for us to walk in. Because that is our life. We sometimes unconsciously brush our teeth, take a shower and eat. We don't have to make an effort to do many things. So also, when we live in the Spirit, the natural outcome is to do good works. Love is life, not concepts. If I have love, I have the life and the fruit of the Spirit.

So if I help the poor because I believe in the concept of helping the poor, that is dead works. But if I help the poor because the love of the Spirit is urging me to do it, then it is of Him. "That which is born of the Spirit is spirit" (John 3:6 NASB). Paul said, "If I give all my possessions to feed the poor, . . . but do not have love, it profits me nothing" (1 Corinthians 13:3 NASB). It is dead works. Good works that are not inspired by God Himself, for me are dead works.

When are we going to learn to be led by the Spirit? We start with life, and then we follow by rules. Someone is converted and God gives him new life. It is beautiful. We praise the Lord! And the older Christians say, "He is new. He is full of fire and speaks to everyone about Jesus. It's going to pass. This is the first love. It won't last." They themselves are bogged down with laws, rules, regulations, creeds and doctrines, and life has stopped.

But life is a continual metamorphosis. It is a continual, dynamic change. There is no end to the growing experience, if we give God a chance.

When I was three years old, I was thinking continually about candies and chocolates. When I was eight I was more interested in bicycles than chocolates. When I was eighteen I wanted a motorcycle, and the bicycle wasn't enough for me. When I was twenty I was going after a car. When I was twenty-six my dream was a house. Now my dream is a farm. What is the difference? Growth, and the change that comes with expanding knowledge and experience.

Life is continual renewal. The cells of our body are continually renewed, or they die. Jesus came that we might have life abundantly. He didn't come to give us a set of rules, but a life, a reality. Only what has spirit has life. Only the Word become flesh is life. Has Jesus, the Word, become flesh in you and me? Are we walking along the way in the Spirit of Christ? Is it His life that is flowing from me—His love? His joy? His peace?

Growth comes when the life of the Spirit begins to take over. One day at a time His manna comes. His love rules today, as we are being led by the Spirit of God. Alleluia!

13

Growing Is Changing

Standing at the door of the church after the Sunday sermon, I heard statements like the following year after year:

"Ah! What a nice message."

"Thank you very much, preacher, it was very good."

"We will come next Sunday to hear another one."

"Very good, pastor."

I heard this a hundred times. It is the custom to say "Very good" and "Thank you." Even if you have preached poorly, they say, "Thank you very much." It encourages you to keep on talking even though they don't hear anything. Many of my members sat in my services year after year, yet their lives never changed.

Every time God speaks, it is to renew our minds in order

to bring about changes in our lives. If that is not happening, we are dull of hearing.

> We have much to say, and it is hard to explain, since you have become dull of hearing. For though by this time you ought to be teachers, you have need again for some one to teach you the elementary principles of the oracles of God, and you have come to need milk and not solid food. For every one who partakes only of milk is not accustomed to the word of righteousness, for he is a babe. But solid food is for the mature, who because of practice have their senses trained to discern good and evil.
> Hebrews 5:11-14 NASB (See also Isaiah 28:9.)

So the first change needed is that of becoming quick to hear. Were the things Paul called hard to explain too deep? No, the readers were dull of hearing. The problem is not the truth. The problem is in us. Our minds are so conditioned by our traditions, and we have heard so many messages that go in one ear and out the other that we are dull of hearing. We hear messages that never produce any change in our lives!

Paul said in very plain words what should happen to Christians: "Be not conformed to this world: but be ye transformed by the renewing of your mind, that ye may prove what is that good, and acceptable, and perfect, will of God" (Romans 12:2 KJV). Do you come out of a service or a time with the Lord transformed by the renewing of your mind? Every time we hear something from God, and really hear it, it will renew our minds and transform our lives. If there is no change in our lives, we were not hearing anything. Every time God speaks, we are shocked, we are renewed, and then we are changed.

The writer to the Hebrews realized that his readers were dull of hearing. Today people are dull of hearing, but many preachers don't know it and keep on speaking anyway.

The writer to the Hebrews next complained that by the time the Hebrews ought to be teachers, they needed someone to teach again the elementary principles of God. If the first step in growth is becoming quick of hearing, the second is to become a teacher, responsible for spiritual children.

Teachers and parents plan for their children. I know how it is with Martha and me. Every first of the month we make a list of the food needed for our children. We must make both ends meet, and we must think also of what they need. They need fish. They need red meat. They need vegetables, both green and yellow. It is not what we like particularly that matters but what we need because we have children. We want them to be bright mentally and physically strong. So when winter comes, we say that vitamin C is needed, and so on. They do not understand that. They would eat candies all day long, just because they are children, not because they are bad. When you have spiritual children, you will think of their need for solid food.

Somehow I was brought into a new realm in the things of God, and the fact is that now I have spiritual sons and they are pushing me all the time for more food. They want more and more.

In many meetings today there are those who are "bastards." No one knows who their parents are. We know they are members because their names are in the file, and they can show their membership card at business meetings. But no one is feeling responsible for them.

We don't do that in my family. We know which are our children. They don't need credentials, they *are ours*. And

114

when you have a family, you know their need for solid food.

If one is to have solid food, he must first be done with milk. Paul says something about milk in 1 Corinthians 3, and Peter explains that milk is sound doctrine, the teaching of life. "As newborn babes, desire the sincere milk of the word, that ye may grow thereby" (1 Peter 2:2 KJV). "Sincere" milk is unadulterated milk. And if you keep reading in I Peter 2 and 3, it tells young believers what to do: how to submit to the government, how servants work, how wives behave, how husbands behave. That is the milk of the Word, the sound doctrine, the teaching of life.

When the writer to the Hebrews talks about leaving milk for strong meat, he says:

Therefore leaving the elementary teaching about the Christ, let us press on to maturity, not laying again a foundation of repentance from dead works and of faith toward God, of instruction about washings, and laying on of hands, and the resurrection of the dead, and eternal judgment. And this we shall do, if God permits.

Hebrews 6:1-3 NASB

The very first milk from the mother's breast that the newborn babe receives is the colostrum. Repentance, faith, baptism, the laying on of hands to receive the Spirit and the waiting for the resurrection and judgment are the colostrum to prepare one for the full milk. The colostrum purges the stomach of all past, unborn things, and prepares it to receive the milk.

In what stage of growth are we? Seven years ago I took a look at all my messages, and asked myself, *What have I been preaching all my life?* For twenty-five years I had been preaching almost the same things: repentance, faith, baptism, the baptism in the Holy Spirit, preparation for the coming of the Lord, the resurrection and the judgment. All my sermons were on these subjects. Even all the Sunday school material was on these basic principles.

My books of systematic theology were all on these subjects. The first chapter was on the Holy Scriptures, the second on God, then the Lord Jesus Christ, then salvation, with repentance, then the Holy Spirit, then the last things—the coming of the Lord, the resurrection and judgment. Full stop. The book is finished. That is the way we have been trained. Of course, in seminaries we use the Greek and Hebrew words. But whether it is Hebrew or Greek, it is on the first principles. No wonder we are children!

I was in Singapore in a school, and the teacher was saying, "You are children. You must have the solid food, you must . . ." He preached tremendously well on this.

But when he finished, I made the mistake of asking him, "Dear brother, could you define what is milk and what is solid food?"

"Well," he said, "milk is milk." Yes, of course. "Solid food is—really, I never thought about it."

How can you give solid food if you don't know what solid food is? We think that solid food is when we preach repentance using the Greek and Hebrew words. Don't fool yourself. That is just colostrum, not even milk yet. Because after repentance comes the teaching on the new way of life: husbands, wives, employees, and citizens are to do this and that.

In order to show you how really underdeveloped we are, there is a movement today that believes in salvation, the baptism of the Holy Spirit, healing, and the second coming of the Lord. And this they call the full Gospel! You see where we are? If we call this the full Gospel, what hope is there for us? If we can put up a sign, "Full Gospel Church," because we preach the first principles, we are stuck. We are not growing because we believe we are already grown!

What does the statement, "leaving the first principles," mean? What is "leaving"? It means leaving. "Bye bye!" Don't be afraid. Let us go on to perfection. Of course, we lay again the foundation every time a person comes to the Lord. But if all of us keep circling around on that, it is a tremendous mistake. You don't put a person in kindergarten for the rest of his life. Only once in your life are you in kindergarten, then on to first, second, and third grades.

Furthermore, the writer says that "every one that useth milk is unskillful in the word of righteousness: for he is a babe" (Hebrews 5:13 KJV). Then in order to have solid food, we must be skillful in the word of righteousness. What is the word of righteousness? You know that there is the written Word and the living Word. The written Word—I am talking now of the Bible, particularly the New Testament—is the picture of the food the apostles received. It pictures food of the past, of the first century. We could say, "Look at this food that God gave to Paul for Timothy! This food that God gave to Paul for the Ephesians is different. The dish He gave for the Corinthians is different still."

But what is the food that God is giving to Johnny for Buenos Aires? I cannot be fed only with pictures of food given to the Corinthians. When I go to a restaurant in America, they give me a bill of fare with all the pictures of the dishes they serve. But then I say, "I want this with sour cream, with french fries, etc." And they bring it. You cannot be fed with the pictures; you need the dish with actual food in order to be fed.

I am amazed at the wonderful, precious food that Paul

ate and that God gave him for others. We can say, "God, I want something like that, like those pictures in the New Testament, but I want the actual food I need today. In Buenos Aires, Lord, we cannot be fed with pictures of food given nearly two thousand years ago to churches with a different culture and situation and status of growth." We need the food, the actual food for today, for our world, for our people. Don't you think so?

I am not saying that the Bible is not relevant for today. Whatever stage of growth we are in, we can usually find our condition pictured somewhere in the Bible. Then the word for that condition may be our word from the Lord. But the Holy Spirit must make the application of any portion of the Scriptures to our hearts. And the Holy Spirit does not have to use the Bible to speak to us. He can convict us, impress us or lead us in a certain situation by communicating directly to our spirits.

And of course, it is tremendous to have the pictures of the food Paul received. And when we receive ours, we can compare them. This is mashed and that was fried, but it is the same doctrine. It's just adapted for today.

Suppose Paul had written, "Dear Timothy, I bought a Plymouth car and it's really wonderful. If you buy a car, buy a Plymouth." Then, using the Bible as we are accustomed to, we would be making a rule that all preachers should have Plymouths. But looking at the spirit of it, you would realize that Paul bought Plymouth cars because they were the best at that time. Today perhaps the Mercedes Benz is the best. So let us buy Mercedes if we want the best. If Paul were here today, he would have to say Mercedes. That is the spirit of the letter.

Why did God give to each of the seven churches of Asia a different message? He could have given one message for all seven. But He said to John, to the church at Ephesus, say this and this and this; to the church at Sardis, say this; to

the church in Philadelphia, say that; to the church of Laodicea, tell them this, and so on (Revelation 2 and 3). Why
was one message not sufficient for all?

There is a written Word and a living Word, and many
times we commit foolishness in our churches. In one city I
went to hear a very good preacher of the Bible—really out-
standing. He taught the whole book of Habakkuk in one
class. I like those studies very much that teach a whole
book.

He told us that in the second chapter it says, "I will
stand upon my watch, and set me upon the tower, and will
watch to see what he will say unto me, and what I shall
answer when I am reproved" (Habakkuk 2:1 KJV). The
preacher talked on what it means to stand upon a watch.
He said, "Brothers, we see how America is today. To stand
upon the watch means fasting and intercession, being in
the place to hear what God has to say to us for today. We
must be concerned with the problems." I thought, *Wonderful!*

Then he kept on teaching, and when he got to the last
verses about rejoicing even when the fig tree does not
blossom, and so on, he said, "Even if America goes down
the tube, we have to rejoice in the Lord; we don't have to
be preoccupied with Watergate or other scandals."

And I wondered, now which shall I do? Shall I go out to
the watchtower to pray and fast? Or should I rejoice with
America going down the tube? He gave two messages in
the same lesson, because it was letter-centered. He did not
know he was giving two different messages, and nobody
said anything because it was Biblical. What was the Spirit
saying to those people? What was the will of God for
them—to pray and fast or to rejoice?

To be skillful in the Word means to be skillful not only
in the written Word, but in the living Word. The living
Word is very sharp.

The writer to the Hebrews says also that solid food belongs to them who are of full age, even those who by reason of use have their senses exercised to discern . . . To discern what? What is good for him and what is bad for him. That is what the Greek really means.

To have our senses exercised does not mean the natural senses—the sight, the hearing, and the smell—but the spiritual senses. Full age means full grown and so we discern what is good for eating.

A child eats whatever he sees, even dirty things. "Don't put that in your mouth!" we have to say continually. He eats dirt. He eats with dirty hands. We have to be careful with little children all the time. But when we are of full age, we know what we can eat and what we can't because our senses of smell, taste and sight are developed.

So, as full-grown Christians, we have the discernment by our spiritual senses. You are warned, "Brother, don't join that person, or those people; they have a false doctrine."

You can answer, "Don't worry. I have my senses exercised to discern what is good and evil."

The anointing which we have received of the Lord abides in us. The senses of the Spirit are able to discern the spirit of other people. We do not have to judge only by the words they say. Perhaps their words are wrong according to our conditioned way of thinking, but the spirit is good. Their motivations are in God. If we are guided only by hearing the things a person says, we might be fooled. But we can go deeper than that. This is why I have fellowship with people of different creeds.

The provider of solid food is God Himself. He is the source of all truth. He is the Way, the Truth and the Life. God Himself said, "I will put My Spirit within you and cause you to walk" (Ezekiel 36:27 NASB). So the source of solid food is in direct dealings with God.

The Roman Catholics are church-centered, or body-centered. It is the Church that decides what people have to believe. Popes have been saying all along that the Church is to interpret the Scriptures and the traditions, and the faithful accept that.

In reaction to this, the Protestant and evangelical churches say, "No. That's wrong. We must be Bible-centered. The Bible is the rule of faith."

Catholics reply, "We cannot be Scripture-centered because it was the Church which determined the canon of Scripture. The Church brought the Scriptures, and it was not the Scriptures that brought the Church."

By Protestant thinking the Bible is the truth, and so we claim to be Bible-centered. Forgive me, I have to be honest with you. Let's say I am a member of a denomination which believes that the Bible is the Word of God. Then I start to speak in tongues, and the leaders say, "Get out!"

"Why?"

"Because we don't believe in tongues."

"But tongues are in the Bible, and the Bible is the rule."

"Yes, but tongues are not our doctrine."

Then, for these Protestants, the church really is the final and last judge of the Scriptures also.

May we not rather be Christ-centered? Truth-centered? The source of truth is God Himself who said, "I will dwell in them, and walk in them; and I will be their God, and they shall be my people" (2 Corinthians 6:16 KJV). The apostles never preached the Bible or the Church. They preached a Person, Jesus Christ. They used the Scriptures when they needed to use them, but the people didn't convert to the church or to the Scriptures but to the living Christ.

The order should be this. First God Himself; second the Church, the called-out ones; third the Scriptures. The living God speaks. If we are in doubt, we check with the

Body. If the Body is in doubt, let us look to the Scriptures and find the closest reference to the situation we are in and see what God's called-out people did then.

If we invert this order, we lower God, putting the Head lower than the Body, or lower than our interpretation of the Scriptures. Let us not limit God nor lower Him.

Are we still hungry for solid food? Then read what Paul says:

> For I determined not to know anything among you, save Jesus Christ, and him crucified. . . .
>
> Howbeit we speak wisdom among them that are perfect: yet not the wisdom of this world, nor of the princes of this world, that come to nought: but we speak the wisdom of God in a mystery, even the hidden wisdom, which God ordained before the world unto our glory: which none of the princes of this world knew: for had they known it, they would not have crucified the Lord of glory.
>
> But as it is written, Eye hath not seen, nor ear heard, neither have entered into the heart of man, the things which God hath prepared for them that love him. But God hath revealed them unto us by his Spirit: for the Spirit searcheth all things, yea, the deep things of God. (Solid food!)
>
> For what man knoweth the things of a man, save the spirit of man which is in him? Even so the things of God knoweth no man, but the Spirit of God. Now we have received, not the spirit of the world, but the spirit which is of God; that we might know the things that are freely given to us of God. Which things also we speak, not in the words which man's wisdom teacheth, but which the Holy Ghost teacheth; comparing spiritual things with spiritual. But the natural man receiveth not the things of the Spirit of

God: for they are foolishness unto him: neither can he know them, because they are spiritually discerned. But he that is spiritual judgeth all things, yet he himself is judged of no man. For who hath known the mind of the Lord, that he may instruct him? But we have the mind of Christ.

And I, brethren, could not speak unto you as unto spiritual, but as unto carnal, even as unto babes in Christ. I have fed you with milk, and not with meat: for hitherto ye were not able to bear it, neither yet now are ye able. For ye are yet carnal: for whereas there is among you envying, and strife, and divisions, are ye not carnal, and walk as men?

1 Corinthians 2:2, 6-16; 3:1-3 KJV

But if ye have bitter envying and strife in your hearts, glory not, and lie not against the truth. This wisdom descendeth not from above, but is earthly, sensual, devilish. For where envying and strife is, there is confusion and every evil work.

But the wisdom that is from above is first pure, then peaceable, gentle, and easy to be intreated, full of mercy and good fruits, without partiality, and without hypocrisy. And the fruit of righteousness is sown in peace of them that make peace.

James 3:14-18 KJV

May God make alive in our hearts the pictures of solid food given us by the apostles. The Holy Spirit will serve us the actual food we hunger for.

14

Ministering the New Covenant

Any seminary can make you a minister of the letter, but only God can make you a minister of the Spirit. To minister letter is to give out verses of Scripture. To minister Spirit is to impart spiritual life. The letter kills, but the Spirit gives life!

And we are confident of this through Christ Jesus, not that we are sufficient in ourselves, but our sufficiency is of God who made us able ministers of the new covenant; not of the letter, but of the spirit (2 Corinthians 3:4-6). What does it mean to be ministers of the new covenant? It is to minister what? Spirit and life. This is the reason Paul says we are not sufficient in ourselves. Our sufficiency comes from God.

The disciples were much used in the laying on of hands

and other faith-communicating acts. Once Paul said to Timothy, "Receive the gift of prophecy!" But Timothy never used it. So Paul wrote, saying, "Come on, don't make me a liar, use it. I gave it to you. You must have it."

Grace is dynamic life, not a word. To impart grace is to give something; not verses, but a living thing; not the shadow, but the reality. Ministers of the Spirit are ministers of the reality. Look at this ministry of the Spirit.

"For," says Paul, "I long to see you, that I may give you some Bibles ..." Oh, no—"in order that I may impart some spiritual gift to you, that you may be established" (Romans 1:11 NASB). What is established? The life of the Spirit in them.

"And I am sure that, when I come unto you, I shall come ... (With a truck full of literature? No!) in the fullness of the blessing of the Gospel of Christ" (Romans 15:29 KJV). This is tremendous! We are looking at a picture of the things we need to experience. Let's keep looking.

And when they had appointed elders for them in every church, having prayed with fasting, they commended them to the Lord in whom they had believed. ... and from there they sailed to Antioch, from which they had been commended to the grace of God for the work that they had accomplished.

Acts 14:23, 26 NASB

Commended to the grace of God. What is the grace of God? The new covenant; the ministration of the Spirit.

You remember Paul and Silas in the jail? They were living under the new covenant. They had the rivers flowing. They had the well springing up, so they just opened the faucet—out flows living water!

They were in the jail and it was the worst time of night—twelve midnight. They had been lashed, blood on their backs. They were tortured and they were singing, "The fruit of the Spirit is life, love, joy, peace, la, la." That's life. A cold letter written on a heart of stone won't do this.

What is it to minister the new covenant? I'll give you an example. When the disciples were sent ahead of Jesus, Jesus gave them some interesting instructions.

"And into whatsoever house ye enter, first say, 'Peace be to this house.' And if the son of peace be there, your peace shall rest upon it; if not, it shall return to you again" (Luke 10:5, 6 KJV). They were to give to the house, not verses on peace, but the peace. Do you see any difference?

When they arrived at a house, they found a couple quarreling. The child was crying. The dog was barking.

Then they came and said, "The peace of God be on this house." The house changed. The husband called his wife "Honey"; the dog wagged his tail; the child was smiling. What happened? They had brought the peace.

"Oh, thank you," they said.

"We are come to tell you that the Messiah is coming along behind us. He sent us out before Him to tell you He is coming."

"What Messiah? I've got too many things to do. I'm not thinking about religion. Get out of here!"

"We'll get out of here, but we will take the peace with us."

"Bow wow!" "Waah, waah . . ." Quarreling begins again and the house is in confusion.

Do you see the difference between giving verses and giving peace? One is the shadow, the other the very reality.

Peter and John were entering the temple, and they found a lame man. He asked for money.

"We have no silver nor gold," they said, "but what we have we give unto you—here we have a portion of the Gospel according to St. Matthew. Take it."

That sounds more like us than like Peter, doesn't it? That's what we do.

But Peter said, "Such as I have give I thee: In the name of Jesus Christ of Nazareth rise up and walk" (Acts 3:6 KJV). They had Spirit and life, not only the letter. Every time I read this wonderful Book now, I am more anxious to experience what it speaks about.

New covenant is the real thing. We say we believe in love. We have the concepts and principles of love, but not the love. We have a conceptual religion. All religions are conceptual. But Christianity is different if Christians observe the fact that Jesus said, "Lo I am with you always!" Jesus is alive! We have life, not concepts.

That is why the primitive people evangelize so soon after conversion. They have no concepts really. They do not see the Bible as a systematic book. They have no commentaries, no manuals. Often they don't even have the New Testament. These poor people only have the Holy Spirit!

Jesus said, "But when He, the Spirit of truth, comes, He will guide you into all truth" (John 16:13 NASB). I think that is clear, isn't it? The Spirit of truth will guide you into all truth. I will tell you a secret—we have not been trusting the Spirit! But Jesus said, "He will guide you into all truth." If I am not misunderstanding, He said that the Spirit we were going to receive will guide you, *will guide you,* into all truth, *all truth!*

Take a large Sunday newspaper with all its sections, and let us say that it represents all the knowledge and wisdom of God. Then take out one section. This represents what was revealed to Paul when he was taken up to the third heaven. When he came back, he knew a certain amount. God didn't reveal it all to him, just a part. And part of this we take out, because he said he was not permitted to repeat that; it was just for himself.

Take out another section to represent what Paul taught

127

when he went preaching. There were no tape recorders then, so we have no cassettes of what he taught. Also the main teaching of Paul was done privately, when he was with people. At some places he stayed two or three years. Three years! How many books could that make? And remember the world could not hold all the books of all that Jesus said and did, if all had been written. But even if all the sermons of Paul had been written, still the main part would be what he gave privately.

The section of the newspaper we have left represents Paul's epistles. These do not contain much of his main teaching, however. Only the epistle to the Romans has some of it. He had not been to Rome, so he wrote everything he could. That is mostly milk. It is on justification and salvation. The other epistles are *corrections* mostly, and by them we can imagine what the main teaching could have been, though it is not there. If the Church had faithfully followed the guidance of the Spirit, they would not have needed the corrective epistles and we would not have most of what we call the New Testament.

So of all the things he said personally, we may have less than half. And we don't have all the epistles. In the "first" epistle to the Corinthians, he talks of a former epistle that was lost. We hear about the epistle to Laodicea. That also got lost. So we have only this much of what Paul wrote. And of the things we have that Paul wrote, we don't understand them all. And of the things we understand, we don't practice them all! So there is a great deal of truth left for us to be guided into!

God grant that we may grow to be quick of hearing to know what the living Lord is saying to us today. We need solid food. We need what Paul said he could only teach among the mature: the hidden wisdom of God that eye has not seen, nor ear heard. God will take us into His fortress and show us the blueprints of His kingdom. He will raise up apostles and prophets, master-builders who have the blueprints of His Church.

How is the life of the new covenant communicated? Jesus did it by walking the dusty roads with people. What better way is there? On one of my trips holding pastors' seminars, an English-speaking Christian accompanied my brother-in-law and me.

After a month, he said, "Johnny, teach me this way. Tell me what's wrong with me."

I just looked at him dumfounded. Finally, I said, "If you haven't learned anything this month by our lives, we have nothing to tell you."

He began to think back. Tears came to his eyes. At last he said, "Oh! I see it. Those new shoes someone bought you, you made sure they were the right size and gave them to your brother-in-law. Someone gave you a coat and that went to him too. Three or four times in the car, I have broken down and wept because you two have reacted to something in a way opposite to how I would have reacted, or any Christian I know would have reacted. Totally different. A totally loving reaction. This is what the Holy Spirit is dealing with me about—my resentments, deep selfishness and pride! Now I know that what you have been saying in the seminars is more than words!"

This brother came to the blood of the cross for cleansing and new life began more fully in him. Jesus showed us that the most important way of passing on life is by living and observation.

Whenever possible, we work as a team. Perhaps the best way is to work in team, as I like to do, with my wife and children, as they are growing up. We live in close to another family. I share with the father, Martha shares with the wife, and my children share with their children. Each of us knows that the important thing is what happens to people on a deep level in coming to the cross.

Also, in my congregation, I took a group of men to be with me. We spent much time together and shared everything. After six or seven months, they were so changed that each automatically found a circle of people around him who wanted what he had. Their neighbors and Christian friends started coming to them with questions and needs. Each of my disciples had a cell group developing out of life and need—not assigned. It took more than two years, by this process, until the whole church was involved in cells, meeting in homes.

I spend as much time as possible with the leaders. At the beginning we started having retreats, very many retreats. Now we have one meeting a week, four hours long, and once a month we go out to the country together from Friday night to Sunday afternoon. We have no more Sunday morning meeting. We thought people should rest on Sunday morning or visit another congregation. Our Sunday evening service gathers everyone together for singing and worship and exhortation. Teaching is not done then, but rather in the cell groups. It is what you might call *didaché* in the cell group, and *kerýgma* on Sunday evening.

When the leaders are together, we are all just Christ's disciples. We become a family, linked together and yielded to one another in love. Many times the brothers teach me tremendous lessons.

I often tell one of them, "Brother, what you say is of God. Let's do as you say." For now they are spiritual fathers, too.

Sometimes one of them checks me, "Johnny, that doesn't sound like the way." And it may well be that in that situation, he becomes the leader. They always retain a respect for me, as I respect my mother, even though I am no longer under her rule now that I am grown.

Be careful not to copy. It is dangerous to duplicate. Every congregation needs its own message, as God revealed a different message to each of the seven churches of Asia Minor in the Revelation of John.

In our congregation on Sundays we were all beautifully dressed, nice and correct. But as God got closer to us, the Spirit began to show us ourselves. We knew we were bad husbands, bad wives and bad children. Everything was confusion in our homes. So we started to seek a way for Him to rule in our homes.

First we saw what each person was in his life. If he was married, he was a husband. If he had children, he was a father. If he had parents alive, he was a son. If he was an employee or if he was a boss—all things in his life were important. So the lessons came.

They were milk. The milk of the Word applies to the life we live. Paul says to Titus:

> Speak the things which are fitting for sound doctrine. Older men are to be temperate, dignified, sensible . . . Older women likewise are to be reverent in their behavior . . . that they may encourage the young women to love their husbands . . . Likewise urge the young men to be sensible . . . Urge bondslaves to be subject to their own masters in everything, to be well-pleasing, not argumentative, not pilfering . . .
>
> Titus 2:1-10 NASB

So sound doctrine is behavior, not our philosophy or our beliefs. When we started to give milk to our people, it changed their behavior, not their beliefs. We found that people of all varieties of denominations and doctrines can come and accept this milk without quarreling, because all believe in the practice of love in God's kingdom. And the way we live is more important to our neighbors than the way we think.

So we try to stress the way of living with our people, that

the world may see our good works (not our good thinking) and glorify our Father in heaven. Jesus said, "Teaching them to *observe* all things that I have commanded you." How can you observe the millennium or the Trinity? Things to observe are practical things.

If we had called these groups home Bible studies, people might have come, read the Bible, prayed, and gone home. We called them cells at first because cells are small, living and they multiply. But now we have changed the name to "small communities." We may change again.

What we do in the cells is to sit together at Jesus' feet, seeking to know His will for us in practical ways. The Holy Spirit shows a problem in the home of one man. He tells us all about it and others share suggestions with him. He comes to the cross in repentance. Next week he comes back saying, "We have had the best honeymoon of our lives!"

All rejoice, and someone else is convicted as he realizes his home is not like that. That day, the blood of the cross meets him, as he deeply bows down in spirit. He goes home and makes things right with the Lord and his family.

This is all on a very practical level and touches all relationships. We are open with each other. We may need to seek the guidance of the Spirit on how to show our love to our wives or husbands. We share on how to make ends meet—someone knows where to buy at wholesale prices. Nothing is too mundane to bring to Jesus and His family. Of course, this kind of learning and ministering the milk to one another is not possible in large meetings on Sunday, but it is effective in cells. Soon everyone around us knows that all these homes are changed and full of joy.

We find people in the small communities become much better Christians in all respects. When we finished putting everybody in small groups, we wanted to see if we could do without the church building. So we shut it down for one month and had meetings in the homes only. That meant we had to change our way of receiving the offerings. When our members started giving their tithes through the cells, the church income doubled, because every member of the cell was giving! In a small group everybody knows everybody and knows how much everybody earns. So when each one had to give the envelope to the leader, everybody tithed!

Speaking of tithing, that is an old covenant concept. When we get into God and everything we have is His, and when we begin to love one another, giving goes way beyond tithing. Our giving is under the joyous guidance of the Holy Spirit.

Not only that, but everybody speaks, everybody confesses, everybody is rebuked when needed, everybody is fed. There is also social involvement—almost like your social security, which we do not have. When one person loses his job, the other people in the cell help him until he gets another job. Of course, they also help a lot in getting him a new job.

When love begins to flow out into the community, people come to know Jesus in ones and twos, sometimes sixes and eights. Many come simply because of what they see happening in the lives of the believers.

As we minister the milk to new believers, our goal is to make disciples. A disciple must be yielded to authority. But we don't want to make a slave out of anyone. We want to make a leader. We don't want to rob people of their initiative and capacities or make them lazy.

If a man is thinking of selling his house and comes to me saying, "Brother Ortiz, shall I sell my house or not?"

I would say, "Ask the Lord."

"But I am under your authority."

"No, you seek the Lord. He will guide you. That is what He promised."

The Lord Jesus Christ, when He started to teach disciples, first bent their stiff necks to His will. He sent them out and told them, "Don't say 'hello' to anybody in the way. When you get to a house, say, 'The peace of God be upon you.'"

"But what if I want to say, 'Good evening'?"

"No, say, 'The peace of God be upon you.'"

"Don't pass from house to house."

"But what if I am offered a better one?"

"No, stay in the first one."

"Heal the sick and eat whatever they give you."

"But what if I don't like that food?"

"Eat it just the same."

"Don't take two purses."

Those were specific instructions because He wanted to break their rebellion at the beginning.

But later He sent them with fewer instructions. He said, "Remember when I sent you out with nothing? Now take even a sword."

At the last He said, "I will send the Spirit of My Father upon you, and each of you will have My mind." That's growth.

If we grow, the plans and instructions that were good for yesterday are not going to be good for today. If we can do with the same methods, the same liturgies, the same books, the same prayers, the same hymns, the same Sunday school curriculum, it is because we are not growing. I remember that my church was thirty years with the same hymnbook! Now in the last seven years we have changed five times, and now we have an overhead projector because no hymnbook is enough. Every day we have new songs, and sometimes we do not even have time to write it out for the overhead projector!

Meetings are different one month after another. New things, new dialog, new experiences, new things to share about the Lord. No more do we hear the same prayer every

Sunday. We do not think now that to be faithful to the forefathers we should be repeating the same things they did. They were pioneers in faith, and if we are to be their worthy children, we will live in the fresh light we are receiving today. These are days of new light.

Now, fasten your seat belts! Tell me! A person who is filled with love, joy, peace, longsuffering, gentleness, goodness, faith, meekness, temperance,—if he is practicing all these, what will you preach to him? What verse of Scripture is left for instructing him? What shall we do on that day when the life of the Spirit of Christ comes to full fruition in all the Body of Christ? (The Spirit so overflows and surpasses the Law and the letter, that you cannot compare!)

May God give us the spirit of wisdom and revelation in the knowledge of Jesus Christ. May He enlighten the eyes of our understanding that we may know what is the inheritance of the saints and the exceeding greatness of His power to us who believe! (Ephesians 1:18, 19).

15

God's Eternal Purpose

If we are ever to understand God's purposes, we must share His vision of His Church. One day Jesus took His disciples up a mountainside to look out with Him over the city. In those quiet moments He imparted to them a little of what was in His heart for the Church.

It was Jesus who said, "I will build My Church." We tend to think in terms of our group in our city and interpret this to mean He will build the Baptists or Episcopalians or Assemblies. But in the light of the Spirit, He shows us that He means *all* the "called-out ones." His heart is yearning over all in the city who have been called out of the kingdom of darkness into the kingdom of God. This fresh understanding of the Church is going to bring us into a new life, a new attitude, and a new way of working.

For Jesus, in His files in heaven, has "The Saints of Glendale" all together. He doesn't have "The Assembly of God in Glendale," or the "Baptists of Glendale." There is only one group, the called-out people who live in Glendale. In heaven they don't say bad words, like *Baptist, Presbyterian,* and such. That is a foreign language!

When we absorb His frame of reference, we too will see in every city only one group of called-out believers. We will see His sorrow and suffering when He sees division and quarreling. But whether believers are in accord or not, He still sees them from a father's viewpoint—they are His family.

So all the called-out people in a certain area belong to the same church. He doesn't see pastors of the "churches" of Boston, but elders, perhaps, of the church in Boston. The Bible speaks of the elders of the church in Corinth. If, then, the pastors in one city are all servants in the one church, in God's eyes, perhaps they should start to think of the possibility of knowing and loving one another. That can come through visits and doing things together.

If all the pastors in the city are pastors in the same church, then, in Jesus' eyes, all two hundred as a body are the elders of that city. This is very important. He sees *all* of them, not some, whether they like it or not. There are many things we have in Christ that we don't know. But as we know more of Him, we come to know our place in relationship to others in the Body.

Let's say someone gets a vision of this and manages to make friends with fifteen pastors of different denominations, and they become very loving with one another. They take their families and go on picnics together and find they can get along pretty well. Then they say, "Brothers, we are the presbytery of this city."

They are not the presbytery of the city before God, nor even a majority. Fifteen, with 185 absent, is not a good showing. That is no quorum.

"But the others don't want to come," they say. Then that is the challenge and the work Jesus gave us. If we say we understand the Body, if we believe in unity, if we have received God's light, then we are the leaven.

You say, "It's so hard for me to be in this dough!" But that's the place for leaven. If we should bring all of the leaven together apart from the dough, then you have this group of leaven all praising and singing in the Spirit. That's nice. But what about the dough?

The presence of the leaven in the dough is like the presence of the parents in the home. My wife says, "Johnny, when you are at home, the children behave differently." I don't say or do anything special; it is just my presence there. So our presence in that city or area where God has put us is important. Let's be patient. Let's pray. Let's keep on knocking at doors, visiting pastors. For Jesus' sake, let us be inclusivists, not exclusivists.

Otherwise there is a danger of forming a "religious council" of the fundamentalists or the charismatics or something else, and this again becomes a structure of power, and someone is its head. We are caught building again what we were trying to avoid. No group of pastors, unless the whole church is there under the Head, Jesus Christ, can refer to themselves as the elders of the city. It is so easy to start in the Spirit and then follow up in the flesh!

Let us resign the great temptation to exercise the power we have to oblige others to do our will. This is a tremendous thing. Perhaps because of my preaching, or because of my travelings, or because of my books, or anything, I gain some status. If I would have gifts of healing and miracles and raising people from the dead, I would have certain influence over people. People would look at me and say, "He's a servant of God." Then what a temptation to use that influence to oblige others to think as I think, or to do as I do.

One of the most tremendous lessons we see in Jesus is that of resigning the use of power. He could have brought all the angels from heaven to fight for Him, but He never did.

If I should take my influence or spiritual authority and say among my pastor friends, "Dear brethren, I am sorry to have to tell you that Dr. So and So is such and such," and thereby I discredit him, that is my first step down from God's presence. It is misuse of power.

Jesus' disciples were like that during their training.

They said, "Jesus, we have found a group that was casting out demons in Your name, but they don't belong to our group so we forbad them." And of course, at that time there was one group that was really the true group—the one with Jesus in their midst.

But Jesus said, "No, if they are not against us, they are for us." Jesus' arms of love reached much farther than theirs. Can we be like Him?

Can we include in our love and working together the leaders of parachurch organizations, such as Campus Crusade, in the leaders' group of the city? Of course. Can we include a woman pastor? Yes! Let her be one of us. Who are we to pass judgment for God according to our interpretation? For Jesus' sake, accept the church as it is and love it as it is, divided or not, wheat and tares. He will do the changing.

You say, "If there is a pastor with a bad testimony in the city, should we accept him?" Of course. We must be identified with the hurting ones. Who is guilty if that pastor has a bad testimony? We ourselves. The church body to which you belong, too. Perhaps if you had been in the right relationship with the other pastors, if there had been a spirit of love among the leaders in the city, he would not have fallen into sin. And when he comes to the group with all his sins, the group can lead him to the cross for healing and changing by their own honest testimony of deliverance. That is the reason why you are there—to offer covering love.

Some people think that sick people should be prohibited from coming into hospitals! If we are ministers at all, we are ministers of reconciliation. So what a wonderful challenge to receive the pastor with the bad testimony in redeeming love. The law came by Moses; grace and truth by Jesus Christ. Grace and truth come in that order—grace first. When we were yet sinners, Christ died for us.

There is a fresh understanding that unity is identification with the called-out people of God. It is unity of spirit, not unity by conformity. It is love. This is not according to my convenience, or whether I agree or disagree with one or another. I don't leave this group because I disagree. We are a group of the called-out people, so we identify with them whether they are nice and pleasant or not. We were accustomed to being aloof and pointing out where each was "wrong." But to see with God's eyes means that I am a part of the whole Body of called-out people.

When Daniel prayed, he did not say, "*They* have sinned. God, have mercy on *them*." He said, "*We* have sinned. Lord, have mercy on *us*." Nehemiah said the same, even though he hadn't sinned himself. But that is identification with a group you love and believe will be changed. Jesus identified Himself with us while we were yet sinners. He made Himself sin for us. Identification is covering love. Without it there is no redemption.

I cannot hold myself aloof from this divided Church. I am part of this quarreling, sectarian Church. I share the guilt of this situation, and I want to lay my life down for its healing. Jesus had to become a close relative to us to redeem us. It was the law of God to marry a person, or adopt him, in order to redeem him or her. Dare I hold myself aloof from His suffering ones? No, they are mine too.

There is hope. And there is something for all of us to do unitedly. For King Jesus is at work in the universe reconciling all things to the Father. His message to our world and to the whole kingdom of darkness is: Repent! Believe the good news! Jesus has unveiled the kingdom of God with its theme of reconciliation to God. Paul said this Gospel is being preached to all creatures under heaven.

Jesus Christ wants to rule in every heart, though many are still in darkness. What is it to evangelize? The word *evangel* means "good news." The good news is not the doctrine of your little church. That is bad news. The good news is that the kingdom of God is at hand for everybody. "Repent from your rebellion! Come under the rule of the King!"

When will this evangelization be finished? I wonder if God the Father ever gets impatient and says, "Son, when are You going to give the Kingdom back to Me."

And Jesus says, "But everybody is not yet under Me, dear Father. So many have not yet allowed Me to overcome evil by My goodness lived in them!"

"But I gave You all the power. Haven't You finished yet?"

"No, not yet. Wait a little more. I want them *all* to have an opportunity."

That is what Peter said: "The Lord is not slow about His promise, as some count slowness, but is patient toward you, not wishing for any to perish but for all to come to repentance" (2 Peter 3:9 NASB).

But one day God will say, "That's enough."

And Jesus will answer, "Yes, You are right, the time is

up. But before the end, let's send a special outpouring of our Spirit. Let's give a real opportunity to everybody. Unfortunately, My people, My witnesses are weak. The religion built up around Me is so organized, so institutionalized, I think We cannot go through those official channels. Let's give the Holy Spirit to all flesh. Not that all are going to be converted. Many, even when they are feeling God's presence, will say no. But at least everybody will have the option. And then the end will come."

All flesh! Do you know what that means? In Argentina "all flesh" is Catholic flesh. In India "all flesh" is Hindu flesh. In Pakistan "all flesh" is Muslim flesh. One of these days something is going to happen. You had better be prepared.

In Buenos Aires we have planned some things for the time of the move of the Spirit with thousands becoming born again. We will need all hands to collect the harvest. We are ready. We will say to a young person, "Leave one year of your university." To another, "Leave your family." And they are ready. We will tell all sorts of people, "Come on and help."

We are ready to put in the church building a big kettle and make a big stew everyday for the workers to eat all together, and go to work all day in our city. We are ready to leave everything when the Spirit moves. Also, if the need comes, we will be ready to live together, and we try it out so we are prepared when the time comes.

Then the sovereignty, the dominion, and the greatness of all the kingdoms under the whole heaven will be given to the people of the saints of the Highest One; His kingdom will be an everlasting kingdom, and all the dominions will serve and obey Him.

Daniel 7:27 NASB.

For it was the Father's good pleasure for all the fullness to dwell in Him, and through Him to reconcile all things to Himself, having made peace through the blood of His cross; through Him, I say, whether things on earth or things in heaven.

Colossians 1:19, 20 NASB.

Then comes the end, when He delivers up the kingdom to the God and Father, when He has abolished all rule and all authority and power.
For He must reign until He has put all His enemies under His feet. The last enemy that will be abolished is death. For He has put all things in subjection under His feet. But when He says, 'All things are put in subjection,' it is evident that He is excepted who put all things in subjection to Him. And when all things are subjected to Him, then the Son Himself also will be subjected to the One who subjected all things to Him, that God may be all in all.

1 Corinthians 15:24-28 NASB.

Jesus was made King of the Universe, that He may gain back what was lost in the rebellion of Satan. He came to earth and shed His blood for this. He is now putting all things under His feet and wants to put the devil under our feet, too. When Jesus puts everything under His feet, and our feet, when everything is again under His crown, when all powers and dominions are again submitted to Him, He is going to give back the kingdom to the Father.

Alleluia! Amen!